WRITE ON, SISTERS!

WRITE ON, SISTERS!

Voice, Courage, and Claiming Your Place at the Table

Brooke Warner

Author of Green-Light Your Book

SHE WRITES PRESS

Published 2019
Printed in the United States of America
Print ISBN: 978-1-63152-670-1
E-ISBN: 978-1-63152-671-8
Library of Congress Control Number: TK

Interior design by Tabitha Lahr

For information, address:
She Writes Press
1569 Solano Ave #546
Berkeley, CA 94707

Contents

INTRODUCTION:

This Is Our Time

What is voice? What empowers women to speak—up, out, boldly, truthfully? And why must women *claim* a place at the table? These questions are at the heart of *Write On, Sisters!*, which is also a clarion call to women to write, to speak and be heard, and to recognize the myriad influences—historical, cultural, economic, emotional—at play when it comes to how we express ourselves and allow ourselves to be heard.

Women are half the world's population, but we do not have an equal voice in the political arena, when it comes to who gets published, or in journalism, where women are still too often relegated to softer beats.[1] Despite measured gains for women in terms of education and employment, the gender gap—"the difference between women and men as reflected in social, political, intellectual, cultural, or economic attainments or attitudes"—is as wide as it's ever been.[2] In her book *Men Explain Things to Me*,

Rebecca Solnit wrote, "Women fight wars on two fronts, one for whatever the putative topic is, and one simply for the right to speak, to have ideas, to be acknowledged to be in possession of facts and truths, to have value, to be a human being." Women today are fighting as we have historically—for equal representation, for our right to be believed and to be heard and to be read. For our place at the table.

It doesn't matter whether you're writing fiction or memoir or poetry or self-help or children's books—the personal is political. This was a rallying slogan from the second-wave feminist movement in the United States, and it's relevant to women writers of all stripes because the political conditions in which we live affect women's voices. Women's voices are at the center of some of our most recent, gripping national firestorms: the #MeToo Movement, Christine Blasey Ford's Senate Judiciary Committee testimony against Brett Kavanaugh, Stormy Daniels's *60 Minutes* interview and tell-all book, and much more.

Because women are too often silenced, because we recognize the effort to silence and the impact of silencing, we inherently bring personal conviction and values to our writing. Audre Lorde, poet, feminist, and civil rights activist, wrote, "When we speak we are afraid our words will not be heard or welcomed. But when we are silent, we are still afraid. So it is better to speak." In her activism, she gave voice to women everywhere, particularly to women of color, who have faced sexism just like their white counterparts, but also racism, stereotyping, undermining, and marginalization of their voices.

Writing is self-expression, and as such, when we

write we give voice to what we think, what we care about, and who we are. When we read a book—or even a post—we take a walk inside the innermost recesses of the author's mind, welcomed into a place so private that the words we read on the page may be words the author has never uttered aloud. How powerful—and intimate—is that?

Author Dani Shapiro has said that voice is courage. As a publisher of women's books and a writing coach who works to support people to express themselves on the page, I often think about this most simple of definitions. So many authors struggle with voice, thinking it's something they have to find or cultivate or grow into. Others cower once they begin a writing project, writing to the wrong audience, tucking their tails between their legs as they abdicate their authority—to the peers they imagine will judge them, the family members they suspect will never forgive them, the critics they conjure up in their minds. The very act of curbing what we want to say for fear that it might not land well with others is the first step we take in turning over our power—and women writers do this more than men.

I've spent the past two decades working with authors, most of them women. I have enough experience with male authors to be able to compare. Yes, men encounter self-doubt. They worry what others will think. They censor themselves, too. But the degree to which women grapple with their doubts, fears, inner critics, outer judges, and so much more is arresting. It's possible that women just talk about what cripples them more, but I don't think so.

The culprit is a little thing called conditioning, which in psychological terms is learning that happens as a result of responses to our actions. The first half of this book examines the four main forms of conditioning that hold women back: historical, cultural, economic, and emotional. As recently as the 1960s and '70s, girls were regularly steered out of intellectually rigorous career choices, encouraged to be secretaries and nurses and assistants. Women who pushed to be part of the conversation were considered uppity, brazen, rude. They still are. Where women's rights are concerned, we're still just emerging from the womb. The #MeToo movement has shed light on a disturbing revelation that most—if not all—women go through life dealing with bouts of feeling emotionally unsafe, walking on eggshells, ignoring or denying their better judgments, feeling as if they have to swallow whatever's dished out, realizing that calling men out for bad behavior will only make them seem as if they're oversensitive or overreacting. Many women still earn less than men, and even those women who have means struggle to prioritize or assert themselves financially when it comes to their creative pursuits.

It takes incredible stamina to face these kinds of resistance and keep pushing forward. Women writers experience resistance in spades, in the form of discouragement, of not being given the same opportunities as men, of having to weather the sexism of the writing world, of being systemically silenced. Given that women face these kinds of challenges disproportionately, we have to give ourselves props for our persistence. Yes, we can look to the past to see how much we've overcome. That so many women write, that we express out loud, that we publish our truths, are signs of our resilience and strength—and a repudiation of a system that's worked hard to keep women's voices unheard.

Throughout the decades and centuries, the idea that women's stories don't matter has been steadily reinforced. Virginia Woolf started an important cultural conversation—and revolution—in 1929, when she wrote *A Room of One's Own*, which argued that women must have both means and privacy in order to write. She also concluded that women of her generation and prior had to overcome their circumstances in order to write, given the expectation that they become mothers and tend to the household, not to mention the fact that they suffered from lack of education, money, and privacy.

Only in the aftermath of World War II, as women entered the workforce in a meaningful way and began to earn their own money, and then following the women's movement of the 1960s, in which women insisted on being heard in new ways, would we experience a profound cultural shift that gave women's voices a more level playing field. Still, the effect of centuries of conditioning people to believe that men's stories matter more is that collectively we believe this notion to be true. This conditioning seeps into our own conscience, manifesting as a sabotaging internal voice that says things like, *Why bother? Who do you think you are?* Insert whatever worst self-doubt or fear comes to mind. It doesn't matter that your rational brain knows otherwise. It doesn't matter if you came of age in the 1970s during the *Free to Be . . . You and Me* era. It doesn't matter if you're a second- or postwave feminist who believes in gender equality. It doesn't matter if you've been in therapy your whole life to overcome the multitiered impacts of being suppressed. You still believe that what you have to say—compared to whatever more authoritative, deserving, qualified, or talented person you're measuring yourself against—matters less. We all do this.

This is why it's so important to speak and to write and to use our voices. There's a famous quote from award-winning novelist Toni Morrison that I cite often: "If you find a book you really want to read but it hasn't been written yet, then you must write it," she said at the 1981 meeting of the Ohio Arts Council. I like to think she was talking to the women in the audience when she said this. When we speak and write, we claim our right to have a voice, to have a say, and therefore to have power. This extends all the way to claiming our place at the table, which is an act of confidence and audacity. Claiming insists. Claiming demands. Claiming means saying, *It's mine and I'm taking it.* Women are conditioned *not* to be this way. We're not supposed to insist or demand or take things without asking—even though men do it all the time. We're supposed to demur, be polite, and wait our turn. Well, enough of that already, because look how far it's gotten us. Any woman who's heard knows there's a cost, but she also knows it's worth it.

I have heard from too many women since the 2016 presidential election that they are too distracted to write, too upset to unleash their creative energies, that they're wasting too much time on social media and spinning their wheels. In 2018, in an open letter to a young activist during troubled times, Dr. Clarissa Pinkola Estés wrote, "What is needed for dramatic change is an accumulation of acts, adding, adding to, adding more, continuing."

When we write, we add to. When we speak up, we add more. When we publish our work for others to see and consume—this brilliant and brave act of intimacy—we continue. So, Sisters, I invite you to read on but also, more important, to write on. This is our time.

Part I

CHAPTER 1:

She Wrote, She Writes

Women are late to the game of writing and publishing, not by choice but by circumstance, by design, by history. For centuries, women's stories were not heard. Yes, a smattering of early women writers existed—the poet Sappho in the seventh century BC; Julian of Norwich, whose 1395 publication, *Revelations of Divine Love*, was the first book in English credited to a woman; Anne Bradstreet, the first American woman to publish a book in 1650—but for those women who dared to write, it was not with encouragement or support. They were going against the grain, bucking expectations, being revolutionary in their pursuit to self-express. I open this chapter in celebration of the many women authors who fought, as Rebecca Solnit articulated in the quote I cited in the introduction, "for the right to speak, to have ideas, to be acknowledged to be in possession of facts and truths, to have value, to be a human being."

In the nineteenth century and earlier, women who wanted to write were hindered by social pressures not to write or faced real barriers to getting their work published in a meaningful way. Jane Austen wrote in small homemade booklets called quires, which were easily concealable, as it's long been speculated that she felt compelled to hide her writing.[1] In 1837, when Charlotte Brontë, at just twenty years old, sent some of her poems to England's poet laureate, Robert Southey, his response was curt and emblematic of the attitude of the times: "Literature cannot be the business of a woman's life and ought not to be," he wrote. Lucky for us, his discouragement did not deter her. In 1861, Harriet Jacobs wrote and published *Incidents in the Life of a Slave Girl*, an early example of what's known now as "slave narrative," though it should be called an autobiography. Jacobs published under a pseudonym and got the work published only when abolitionist Lydia Maria Child agreed to write the preface.

History books make clear the gendered roles women were expected to adhere to in every arena of life, so it's nothing short of a miracle that some women were able to write and publish at all, given the ways in which they were systematically shut out of public life. Education for white women was limited to upper-class families, and even then, well-educated women were seen as subversive or meddling in men's affairs. The first girls' high schools in the United States opened in New York and Boston in 1826. Women of color were still often seen as chattel, and white women had no political agency and would not earn the right to vote until 1920. In fact, feminist scholars suggest that white women of all social classes were so tied to their husbands prior to the twentieth century that they barely even counted as people.

Charlotte Perkins Gilman's famous 1882 short story, "The Yellow Wallpaper," is an early work of feminist literature that, according to the Conversation, "illuminates the challenges of being a woman of ambition in the late nineteenth century." Gilman's story exemplifies how white women who sought higher education or a creative life—or even read too much fiction—"could be accused of flouting female conventions and placing themselves at risk of mental illness."[2]

Gilman was writing at the very beginning of what's known now as the progressive era (1890–1920), a time when women were fighting to change the very definition of womanhood. Kate Chopin's 1899 novel, *The Awakening*, featured a female protagonist, Edna, whose progressive views and dissatisfaction with her roles as wife and mother make her seem like a very normal and even boring modern-day protagonist. Edna does not behave according to the social norms of the time and kills herself at the end of the book, after her husband leaves her because of her seeming inability to conform.

Despite or because of its depressing ending, *The Awakening* is credited with ushering in a chorus of bolder and louder female voices. The early twentieth century saw the birth of a whole new form of writing called modernism, in which women explored bold topics, such as lesbianism and sexual freedom, rejected domesticity, and paved the way for a new kind of woman writer, such as Virginia Woolf, Zora Neale Hurston, and Gertrude Stein, to emerge.[3] In her book *Writing Beyond the Ending*, Rachel Blau DuPlessis described how women of this era began to venture past conventional story endings of marriage or death. She analyzed the ways in which writers such as Woolf, Dorothy Richardson, Hilda "H. D." Doolittle, Zora Neale Hurston, Muriel Rukeyser, Adrienne Rich, Alice Walker, and others used oppositional strategies to question dominant ideologies. She wrote that "narrative in the most general terms is a version of, or a special expression of, ideology: representations by which we construct and accept values and institutions."[4] DuPlessis speaks directly to conditioning in these lines, iterating the link between self-expression (or historic lack of self-expression on the part of women) and what we accept as our dominant worldview.

As I mentioned in the introduction to this book, Woolf herself must be credited for having started the conversation in *A Room of One's Own*, published in 1929, about how women were discouraged from writing because of circumstance (in effect, conditioning), as well as external and structural barriers to writing, represented by the figure of the Beadle, an Oxbridge (Woolf's fictional composite of Oxford and Cambridge) security officer who reminds Woolf's narrator that only "fellows and scholars" are permitted on the grass; women must remain on the gravel path.

Musing on the inequity of men's and women's experiences, Woolf wrote, "[T]hinking of the safety and prosperity of the one sex and of the poverty and insecurity of the other and of the effect of tradition and of the lack of tradition upon the mind of a writer, I thought at last that it was time to roll up the crumpled skin of the day. . . ."[5]

A decade after Woolf penned her renowned essay, World War II ushered in a new dawn for women. Because women were needed in the workforce, they experienced a profound and collective and unprecedented claiming—of money, autonomy, and also voice. A new kind of woman writer emerged—those who laid the groundwork for contemporary fiction and poetry. Some of the most influential voices of this generation include Doris May Lessing (b. 1919), Maya Angelou (b. 1928), Adrienne Rich (b. 1929), Flannery O'Connor (b. 1925), Joyce Carol Oates (b. 1938), Margaret Atwood (b. 1939), and Toni Morrison (b. 1931). A whole new crop of women writers has come of age in the wake of these literary giants, more influential and numerous thanks to the work of these foremothers.

I would be remiss not to mention the rise of memoir, the genre of my heart, but it wasn't until the 1990s that its trailblazers, in the form in which we know memoir today, appeared. A few of the better-known contemporary memoirs by women are Mary Crow Dog's *Lakota Woman* (1990), Jung Chang's *Wild Swans* (1991), Mary Karr's *The Liars' Club* (1995), and Caroline Knapp's *Drinking: A Love Story* (1997). Popular autobiographies, like Maya Angelou's *I Know Why the Caged Bird Sings* (1969), were published prior to this surge, but these slice-of-life personal memoirs only really began to see a surge in the early 2000s and culminated in the form of such best sellers as *First They Killed My Father*, by Loung Ung; *A Mighty Heart*, by Mariane Pearl; *The Glass Castle*, by Jeannette Walls; *Eat, Pray, Love*, by Elizabeth Gilbert; and *Wild*, by Cheryl Strayed, all of which went on to become films.

The Gatekeepers of the Status Quo

In the twentieth century, there was one way forward for a writer who wanted to be published: getting the blessing of a gatekeeper, the person whose job it was at a publishing company to say yes, we want to publish your book. There are two ways to look at the gatekeepers of the written word: as the people who decide what gets published, or as the people who decide what doesn't get published. Which kind of author you end up being—the one who gets chosen or the one who gets rejected—will likely inform some of your thinking about the role of gatekeepers.

Because I'm a former gatekeeper, and still one, though a 2.0 version who's made a concerted effort to judge books on the merit of their content, rather than on what else an author may or may not bring to the table (e.g., celebrity, followers, etc.), I understand the unique power gatekeepers hold. They're not just decision makers; they're also arbiters of what our culture holds dear who influence what people read by the very act of choosing what gets published.

But who are these people? Historically, they were white men who never confronted the kind of public pressure we see gatekeepers today grappling with—specifically, to be inclusive, to publish more diverse books, to think beyond their own immediate experience when considering what books to acquire. Today, they're mostly white women who do grapple with these pressures, yet, because publishing is so white and still dominated primarily by white men at the top, the trickle-down culture of the industry still reinforces a particular status quo—that the books that really matter are (mostly) authored by white men.

In a 2015 blog post, Hugh Howey wrote that gatekeepers are bad for literature: "They stifle. They censure. They play it safe." I agree with him. They do all these things, but for reasons they might justify. They stifle because they truly believe they know best what sells, based on a very white paradigm; they censure because they want to stay in their comfort zone and thus don't explore options that fall outside the realm of their own known experience; and they play it safe because they often don't have the supporting data (in the form of strong sales of previously published books) to support the risks they might otherwise take. Acquiring a book requires editors to imagine the readership, and if they can't, or if the publisher doesn't know how to reach that readership, then the buck stops there. It's not a good investment if the project requires the company to work its way into unknown territory.

In publishing circles, there's talk about readers being the new gatekeepers. The rise of independent publishing and of books that are finding their readership supports this idea. This is good for women writers, writers of color (men and women), and indie authors, too. Readers read what they like, and one of the great lessons I've learned from independent publishing is the degree to which taste varies. People crave all sorts of stories and all sorts of voices. Gatekeepers are looking for that special something, and today more than ever they're trained to scout fame over talent. But that special something is and always has been subjective, and the gatekeepers often pass over books that go on to sell in huge quantities and change people's lives. So, yes, these people have influence, but authors should never turn over their power to them, because they're not always right and they don't always know best.

The Whiteness of the Publishing Industry

Just how white book publishing actually is was met head-on in 2016 with the release of a Diversity Baseline Survey by Lee & Low Books, which asked publishing houses and review journals to report on the following measures of their employees: race, gender, sexual orientation, and disability. What followed was a conversation about the "diversity gap" in publishing and the revelation (perhaps not so shocking to anyone in book publishing) that the industry is 86 percent white. In a panel I moderated at BookExpo 2018 on this very subject, One World editor Chris Jackson shared that too many of his black counterparts in book publishing had left their jobs out of sheer frustration—about their ideas not being heard, about the glacial pace of change.

Historically, white male gatekeepers have published white male authors, white women and men of color have been the outsiders, and women of color have been the extreme outsiders because of "multiple jeopardy," dual (and sometimes more) and systematic discriminations based on race and gender.[6] But since gatekeepers have always faced economic pressure to perform and to make money for their publishing houses, there have, along the way, been surges in what today might be classified as diverse literature. One such occurrence was during the Harlem Renaissance, which, while driven by a black intellectual movement, was amplified because of white patronage. Langston Hughes credited his patron Carl Van Vechten for an introduction to gatekeeper Alfred A. Knopf, which was the stepping-stone that led to Hughes's work being published in *Vanity Fair* and to his making a living as a poet.[7]

The 1950s and '60s gave rise to a publishing phenomenon known as lesbian pulp fiction. The demand for these paperbacks was through the roof, and countless publishers jumped on the bandwagon. Fawcett Publications stands out in this genre for its conscientiousness (or maybe the company was just invested in the authenticity of the stories) in making a point of publishing lesbian pulp written by lesbian authors, rather than by heterosexual men.

It's hard to know how much certain editors or houses championed diverse writers for diversity's sake. They hardly faced the same pressures editors face today, not just to stay ahead of trends but also to stay fresh and interesting and discerning. It's easy for acquisitions editors to fall back on what they know. Book publishing gets a lot of criticism for being myopic, and there's a reason for that, too. You have a high concentration of publishers in a small space—like New York City—and most of the gatekeepers are well educated, primarily white, and more affluent than the majority of the country. This tends to breed a certain kind of insularity that's hard to avoid unless editors and publishing houses make it part of their mission to be more expansive and far-reaching in their vision.

Since the Lee & Low Books survey, *diversity* has become a publishing buzzword. While people are certainly talking about the topic, questions loom about whether any change is being effected as a result. I asked writer Kwame Alexander, in a November 2018 interview for the podcast I cohost, if he thought things were getting better when it came to diversity in book publishing, and his response was to turn the question inside out. In essence, he said yes, it's an important topic and diverse books do exist, but does the conversation really matter if it's not making an impact on people's lives, if those diverse books are not on the shelves of the people who most need to be reading them? These are good questions to ask ourselves. How are we living our commitment to diversity, rather than just talking about it?

Beyond people's buying habits or the ways in which they're integrating diverse writers into their reading lists and libraries, book publishers reinforce historical conditioning, in the form of what they publish, the people to whom they pay astronomical advances, and whose stories they lift up. A *New Yorker* story, "A Suspense Novelist's Trail of Deceptions," that broke in 2019 epitomizes a problematic and old-school mentality that prevails in book publishing. The magazine profiled Dan Mallory, whose 2018 psychological thriller, *The Woman in the Window,* published under the pseudonym A.J. Finn, had gone to auction in 2016 and sold to William Morrow, the very publisher Mallory worked for, in a two-book, $2 million deal. The *New Yorker* exposé is a long and fascinating piece about Mallory's sociopathic behaviors, illustrated by pathological lying about things that never happened but which elicited the sympathy of others (and which ultimately catapulted him into favorable situations), including his mother's cancer, his own cancer, and surgeries he most certainly never had. Beyond the lying, he had a penchant for snubbing people he didn't like and made his colleagues uneasy. But over and over again, people said, they liked his writing. His emails were good, many colleagues said. And his writing is by all accounts great, except that its storylines are lifted from other bestsellers, something which Mallory has not acknowledged and about which his publisher remains mum.

For all his problematic behavior, Mallory was crowned publishing's latest "it" boy by virtue of all the ways in which the higher-ups at William Morrow fussed over him, not the least of which was his high salary and enormous advance, which trickled out and into the industry at large. Countless people who speculated on this story pointed out how Mallory's ascension in book publishing highlights an industry hell-bent on cultivating young white men like him. Laura Sebastian wrote on Twitter:

> @sebastian_lk
> The Dan Mallory story is wild and hilarious until you remember that young women of color are leaving publishing in droves while mediocre white men continue to find enormous success while making subzero effort and creating hostile work environments for their coworkers.

Sebastian is right to call out this inequity, this double standard, and this injustice for what it is. Book publishers have to do better if they want readers to take seriously their desire to create a more inclusive industry. We have a publishing culture that hails, prioritizes, and lifts up white male authors above all others. Some might argue that, for better or worse, this trend only mirrors the culture at large, but if book publishers want to continue to be the arbiters of what we value as a culture, they must steer, rather than stagnate. Perhaps exposés like the *New*

Yorker's will cause the proverbial scales to fall from the eyes of publishers like William Morrow, which not only propagate the status quo but actually work against inclusivity by harming other, more deserving publishing professionals and authors alike, who feel ostracized in environments that make excuses for—and often reward—bad behavior.

How Women Are Reviewed

In a 2016 interview, Elizabeth Gilbert relayed to me her take on how critics received her novel *The Signature of All Things*. She speculated that it would have been better received in certain literary circles had she not written *Eat, Pray, Love* (which has sold more than ten million copies) first. Somehow, her memoir's extraordinary success had made her less worthy of serious literary accolades, the kind reserved for her male contemporaries, like Jonathan Franzen, David Foster Wallace, or Dave Eggers. Evidence of the kind of disdain she's talking about is palpable in the *New York Times* review for her novel, in which Janet Maslin wrote of Gilbert's fictional protagonist, "She would never have read the 19th-century equivalent of Ms. Gilbert's *Eat, Pray, Love.*"

Reviews are a tricky thing to dissect because they're so subjective. The people writing them, sometimes professional book critics, oftentimes not, absolutely have their own literary preferences and tastes. And while reviews are incredibly important to a book's success, the fact that they're also riddled with inherent bias means they do their part to contribute to the status quo.

In a 2012 article for the *Atlantic*, "Book Reviews:

A Tortured History," Sarah Fay listed the many established authors who've lamented the role of the review in literature dating back to Edgar Allan Poe. She wrote, "One popular complaint is that book reviews are merely a byproduct of the publishing industry and therefore stink of mediocrity, elitism, nepotism, or all three." She also described the recent trend of authors complaining that reviews are too mean, citing a James Wood–Zadie Smith "smackdown" in 2001, in which the famed literary critic wrote a piece for the *Guardian* taking issue with a whole class of modern novel that he dubbed "hysterical realism" and citing Zadie Smith as one of the offenders.

Although Wood's criticism wasn't limited to women writers, he ended the article by saying that he hoped "a space may now open . . . for the kind of novel that shows us that human consciousness is the truest Stendhalian mirror, reflecting helplessly the newly dark lights of the age."

Smith penned her own *Guardian* piece in response, noting the challenge inherent in what she contends is "largely a matter for the intellect." Though her piece waffles between defiance and justifying her position, it ends, in my opinion, on concession: "Your brain must be up for it, for making that necessary leap. At the moment, my brain feels like catfood. So I may never prove to be much of a writer—a real writer, the kind I like to read—but then again, maybe I will. I'm not sure how much it matters anymore. But we shall see."[8]

It's hard to know what Smith's intentions were here. Was she conceding, as I interpreted? Or might this be an attempt at false modesty or a simple emotional defense of her novel? Regardless, this is Zadie Smith, one of the best-loved women authors of our time, responding to a male book critic, showing a kind of vulnerability we see often in women writers and rarely in their male counterparts. And I can't help but wonder whether any of the male writers James cited as guilty of writing hysterical realism would have felt the need to defend themselves by suggesting that perhaps they weren't intellectually rigorous enough, or by ending a similar public response on such a defeatist note.

Women writers contend with a unique kind of scrutiny in that writing is held to a male standard, and as such women are judged by that measure—for how feminine or not feminine their voice or their writing is. And this phenomenon is hardly unique to writing; in fact, twenty-first-century political examples might better explain it.

Let's look at Hillary Clinton's presidential campaign and Christine Blasey Ford's testimony before the Senate Judiciary Committee. Clinton was never allowed to be angry or outraged, not during her run for Senate and not in her shot at the presidency. Every time she spoke too loudly into the microphone, the media chastised her for being "shrill," a word we apply only to women's voices. Rebecca Traister, author of *Good and Mad: The Revolutionary Power of Women's Anger*, wrote in a 2017 article for the Cut, "Censorious anger from women is a liability; from men, it is often, simply, speech." When then-senator Clinton showed an authentic display of emotion on the campaign trail in 2008, welling up in response to a question while sitting in a coffee shop in Portsmouth, New Hampshire, the extreme media shitstorm that followed exemplified how the very act of a woman politician crying was wrong no matter what. Some speculated that Clinton had cried to manipulate, others that this vulnerable moment illustrated how she had just been crafting a cold, hard persona all along and had thus misrepresented herself, and others still that crying simply showed her weakness. In a 1999 study called *The Natural and Cultural History of Tears*, Tom Lutz wrote of political candidates, "The men who cry prove that they are not too manly; the women who maintain stoic control of their emotions prove that they are not too 'feminine.'" This sounds like a big lose-lose for women. Men are allowed to cry; women are not. Men can lose control of their emotions; women cannot.

In 2018, Christine Blasey Ford was in the public eye for only four hours, yet the lessons we can take as women from her experience and the events that followed reinforce the notion that a woman's truth doesn't hold a candle to male power. Blasey Ford was demure, soft-spoken, and seemingly guileless. She was competent, no question, but also tentative at times. If she'd displayed even one-quarter of the intensity or bombastic behavior Brett Kavanaugh showed in his later testimony, she would have been written off as a candidate for institutionalization. Beyond all the detractors who didn't believe her or chose not to, Blasey Ford was criticized for her speech, scorned by some for trying to manipulate or distract with her tone of voice, her "vocal fry"—a way of speaking that's low pitched and characterized by rough or creaking sounds. A 2014 study found that women are judged much more harshly for vocal fry than men.[9] Another study found that men actually exhibit more vocal fry than women, but it's less detectable and/or doesn't come with the same negative associations (like ditziness or incompetence).[10] I can't imagine how nerve-racking it must have been to be in Blasey Ford's position, but I felt frustrated by her demeanor, too. I imagine she chose to take a meek approach, perhaps understanding that her credibility hinged on being the most palatable version of herself she could be, bland enough for Trump to call her a "very fine woman" and "compelling."

Women always lose when we attempt to measure ourselves against a male standard. And even though women have long fought for equal treatment, the fact of centuries of male dominance is nearly impossible to unravel, not least because many men aren't interested in seeing it unravel. Those in power are unlikely to relinquish it in the name of fairness.

In the writing world, fairness is what's at stake. The terrain of female writership is measured not only against a male standard, but also for the very fact of its femaleness. In "Women Writers and the Double Standard," Elaine Showalter discussed how women writers struggled during the Victorian era because "the associations of 'woman' and the associations of 'writer' were too far apart to be connected without strain." This divide resulted in the invention of new names for women writers, including "authoress," "female pen," "female writer," and "lady novelist," all of which allowed women writers to claim their literary ambitions but kept them in check hierarchically. These terms, Showalter noted, "served as constant reminders that [they] were a separate and inferior species of artist."[11]

The women writers of this era pushed back against unequal treatment by writing and submitting their work and getting published. This was not only an act of resistance but also fueled by their desire to express themselves and by their ambition. As the women novelists of this era were published more and more, they began to resist other ways, too. They didn't want special treatment, which was happening in literary circles where women were being reviewed not as authors but instead as authoresses, female writers, and lady novelists.

According to Showalter, in insisting that they be reviewed fairly, for their work, women were defying the "feminine ideal and all its restrictions." Their rationale was simple: judge our work based on its merit, not on the gender of its author. But there were other hurdles to overcome, like the fact that literary ambition was not "respectable." Showalter also wrote, "From childhood, girls were taught that women were created inferior to men in body and in mind, and that God had commanded woman to submit to masculine mastery in return for economic, emotional, and spiritual protection and guidance." In essence, "respectable" women would know better than to risk losing the protection and guidance of their fathers and their husbands by trying to establish their own mastery in the literary realm.

To unlearn this kind of belief is one thing; to defy it is another altogether. And the women of the Victorian era were indeed defiant. George Eliot was one of the leaders of this push for more equal treatment, even while she wrote under a male pseudonym to get her work out more broadly. Then, as now, women writers faced extraordinary scrutiny and often personal attacks. Because motherhood was the ideal to which women were held, women writers were better received if and when they were mothers. Because women's writing was so devalued, women could never abandon domestic duties to focus on their writing; indeed, no woman of that era had a "room of one's own," and Virginia Woolf wouldn't be around for another hundred years to suggest any woman should.

Today, many women have a room of their own, but, just as in Woolf's time, women who have the luxury to choose to write are those with means and agency. Women still must have money and support and dedicated space to make their mark as writers. What we have in spades today are role models—women writers who are celebrated and honored for their work, who write best sellers and make a living as writers. Plenty of women sell lots of copies of their books, though very few of us (very few writers generally) have the luxury of subsisting on our writing alone. We face many fewer restrictions and limitations as women writers, but we have not yet untangled ourselves completely from certain expectations that truly are vestiges of another era. Motherhood is still a measure of a woman's worth. Women are still misunderstood for their literary ambitions. Women still have to fight for equal treatment, and should be, as Elizabeth Gilbert is, skeptical of how their work is reviewed. Women still apologize and qualify. Women still have to fit themselves into a male paradigm of power that doesn't benefit or suit us.

We've achieved so much, yet we have so much further to go. Every single word we write, every single woman writer we champion, and every single expectation we buck is a step in the right direction.

CHAPTER 2:

Writing Under the

Influence of Gender

If you're a woman and you want to write, you must be prepared to endure. Writing is already an endurance test. To write well, to put in the time, to carve out the space, to find it within you to articulate the words you want to say, to share those words, to publish your thoughts and ideas—all of this, while exciting, is also grueling and overwhelming at times. But when you're a woman, there's an added layer of endurance, which involves contending with the fact that the larger culture may not always have your back. Your ideas may be relegated to the realm of "things women care about" or seen as not serious, or not "crossing over" to a male audience.

Women writers navigating the waters of gendered treatment have two choices: to pretend there are no gender differences, in which case you may have a more happy-go-lucky experience (after all, ignorance is bliss), or to tackle some of these inherent problems and biases head-on, perhaps with the goal of participating in the conversation and of effecting change. I understand that some writers prefer to stay blind to gender bias because it's easier or, arguably, because of conditioning. Countless women of certain status insist that gender bias is not a big deal or doesn't impact their experience. This is the very definition of privilege. But if you want to be an advocate for women, it's imperative to bear witness to women's truths. Just because all women aren't experiencing something firsthand (abuse, discrimination, condescending attitudes, slights) doesn't mean it's not happening, and if you're lucky enough to have escaped these situations yourself, it doesn't mean they're not detrimental to women collectively.

In late 2018, I gave a talk about some of the barriers women writers face, touching upon inherent biases against women's work. A sweet author in the audience came to speak to me afterward, gushing about how no one in her life was making her feel less than, how every single person was supportive of her endeavor, and how the only reactions she was getting to becoming an author were positive. This is wonderful, and I was happy to hear this feedback from her, but let's take this author's book as a case study. She wrote a nonfiction book about grandparenting and about how to cultivate a relationship with your grandkids. I've read it, and it's fantastic, but it would be naive to think that grandparenting as a subject isn't relegated to the umbrella category of "things women care about." Should men read her book? Yes! Will some men read it? I'm sure. But when it comes to positioning her book for the market, the publicity hits she gets, and her responses from readers, the experience will be a very gendered one.

I want to be clear that I don't take issue with gendered books. I spent the eight most formative years of my career at a women's press where our mission was exactly that—to bring into the world books for women by women. It was that mission that led to my cofounding She Writes Press. And *this* book is a book for women—no two ways about it. My point more broadly has to do with how our culture marginalizes women writers. And since we're talking about conditioning, it's important to realize that women buy in. We contribute to the status quo because men and women alike subscribe to broader cultural and social values that define it. The reason books are even written *for* women—as an audience separate from men—is that as a culture we believe that women's issues are distinct from men's, that what women care about is different than what men care about. It's a truism in book publishing that books by women are for women, while books by men are for everyone.

Since I work with women writers and spend lots of time in the company of women, I see how women perpetuate some of the very cultural problems I identify in this chapter, mostly because we're socialized that way. The reason men speak up more is that they're encouraged to do so from an early age. Men also do a better job with rejection, insofar as they are less likely to take "no" as a closed door and tend to resubmit at higher rates than women writers do after they've been turned down. Men's books occupy a more prominent space in our culture because of historical precedent, but there are things we can and should do to change that. We can all do better to read more books by women writers and to encourage the men in our lives to do so as well; we can expose the children in our lives to literature by women; and we can elevate those authors we care about, by letting them know when they've made an impact and also by sharing their work, in the form of spreading the word off- and online.

Whereas the preceding chapter touched upon historical treatment of women authors and how that continues to reverberate today, this chapter will look at cultural conditioning and some of the ways in which we can begin to erode it. Because conditioning is learned, it gets internalized, and so we must be vigilant in recognizing it. Pay attention to how women writers are reviewed, what is said about women writers in the media, and the language people use when they talk about women's books. Stand up for women writers if you hear people criticizing the woman behind the book for who she is, rather than for what she wrote. The less we collectively tolerate this slippery slope couched as "literary criticism," the more we will lift ourselves up.

The best antidote I know of for unequal, gendered treatment is to support other women writers. When you see a negative review, employ critical thinking. If you find yourself disliking a particular woman writer, ask yourself why. Is it about her, who she is and her experiences, or is it actually about the writing? If you envy a woman writer because she's doing what you want to do, or because she's achieved some level of success you aspire to, flip the script and consider what might happen if you were to align yourself with her and become a fan. The writing community is small, and we have unprecedented access to writers because of social media. We do actually get to engage and be part of the author community as authors, and when you decide to be generous and support those authors you admire (even if you envy them), those gifts will come back to you when your time comes. I've always found strength in seeing things for how they are, then resolving for myself to participate in hard conversations, to refuse to accept the status quo, and to double down on my support of women writers who are on the path. I hope these are the takeaways you'll find in this chapter, too.

Don't Swallow It

Because of the celebritization of traditional publishing, the industry looks a whole lot more like Hollywood than it has in decades past. Although publishing has always been a gentlemen's club, authors today more than ever are considered and judged as much as or more for who they are than for what they write. And "who we are" and what we get judged for look a lot different for women than for men.

A 2017 Pew Research study offers a window into our modern values and expectations of men versus women. Qualities valued most in men are honesty/morality, professionalism/financial success, and ambition/leadership, while those valued most in women are physical attractiveness, empathy/nurturing/kindness, and intelligence. At the very bottom of the list for women are independence/self-reliance and strength/toughness.[1]

These values manifest themselves in countless arenas of life, but where they intersect with book publishing matters to women writers because we don't get to escape our femaleness, nor can we sidestep the fact that our efforts will be judged through the lens of our being female. Just as is the case in Hollywood, publishing values a woman's appearance more than might seem appropriate, given that content is supposed to be the most important feature of books. In my previous book, *Green-Light Your Book*, I wrote about my experience as an acquiring editor at Seal Press, and how I witnessed a subtle shift over time as the press shifted from approaching acquisitions in a purely editorial content–based manner to a more marketing-oriented, author-focused strategy. We started having conversations in our editorial meetings about whether or not an author was "mediagenic," a euphemism for attractive, or at least attractive enough to be on television and/or have her face plastered across social media.

What I witnessed there was how our collective values were showing up in my workspace in ways that hadn't been visible to me before. Ultimately, this was part of the reason I left traditional publishing, a story I tell in my TEDx talk, "Green-Light Revolution." I was disheartened by the books I could not acquire, especially in comparison with the books I was encouraged to acquire. When I faced a moment at Seal Press when I was actively discouraged from acquiring a book I really believed in, about nontraditional families, and a few months later was given the go-ahead to make the biggest offer of my career for a manuscript about makeup and how to look young and vibrant after fifty, which I didn't think was all that meaningful, I saw it as symbolic. I said in my talk that these two experiences epitomized all the things I'd come to dislike about the industry's decision making—"a value of fluff over substance and rejection of an underserved audience and acceptance based on celebrity and image."

Social media and our me-focused culture play a role in all of this—but we also buy in. We eat the messaging right up. We swallow it whole. We're living in a culture that tells us that the highest measure of a person's worth is his or her fame or celebrity or brand. If we want to write and be successful at it, a bit of a reckoning has to happen. As women, in particular, we have to consider who we are and where we are in our lives and decide how best to approach the burden of these cultural values, because one thing we can't do is will them away.

I was fascinated by the 2016 documentary film *Author: The JT LeRoy Story*, about Laura Albert, who invented the fictional character JT LeRoy, who went on to become one of the hottest literary sensations of the 2000s. The movie showcased how an entire industry got swept up in the latest "it" author, even though JT LeRoy was a fabrication of Albert's mind. If you believe Laura's account of what happened, LeRoy was born out of necessity. Laura herself could never have become an "it" author because she embodied all the surface qualities book publishers shun: She was heavy, unattractive, and self-conscious. While LeRoy's books certainly stood on their own merit, their success was based fully on the myth of who LeRoy was: a gender-fluid youngster with a history of sexual trauma whose edginess made him all the more attractive to the industry.

Laura's story showcases how limited women's options are when it comes to breaking down barriers to getting their work published. If Laura Albert had pitched herself to publishers as Laura Albert, they wouldn't have been able to see past her and into the very writing that launched JT LeRoy to celebrity status. A *New Yorker* review of the film opined that there was a "paternalistic and maternalistic impulse that led to [the industry's] virtual (and sometimes literal) embrace of LeRoy." More interesting to me is the degree to which LeRoy's writing was celebrated because of who he was, and how Laura had the foresight to know that she could never be similarly celebrated, solely because of her outward appearance.

Laura's story is a bit extreme, albeit exemplary. My advice to women authors is to be clear-eyed about gendered criticism and hit back where you can. When a *New Republic* article eviscerated Ariel Levy for who she is—white, privileged, boring—Levy didn't flinch: "I think it would be difficult to argue that I'm a net-negative for womankind. I've tried pretty hard to bring in unusual female voices and perspectives. Not just young women and not just white women, either. I don't know that I'm the best target for improvement. I don't know that I'm the problem."

It's valuable to keep in mind that you might be hit from any side when you're a woman who writes. You will be hit by other women, by people who don't like you or what you represent, and by the industry, with its unconscious bias. I love that Levy took this kind of critique in stride and kept rolling. May you have similar strength and gumption if you find yourself being denounced for who you are, rather than what you've written.

Women's Issues

More times than I care to count during my tenure at Seal Press, I found myself signing off on files with the following category emblazoned across the back cover: "Women's Issues." Classification is a necessity in book publishing. Categories help booksellers, librarians, and readers alike to know what a book is. Categories help to position and sell books. At the same time, there's an inherent problem with categories, in that that they categorize and therefore limit.

I know a lot of women writers who are exasperated by women's categories, especially in fiction, of which there are currently three: African American/Women; Mystery & Detective/Women Sleuths; and the broadest, Fiction/Women. They make the valid point that this kind of labeling is a double standard because there are no comparable men's fiction categories, which emphasizes how the industry sees women's writing as being for women and men's writing as being for everyone. I will also note that designating "African American/Women" is uniquely problematic, as it effectively cordons off black women writers and subjects and no equivalent category exists for black men. Women writers want to be taken seriously as writers, of course—not to be categorized, or relegated, as many see it, to being women writers, rather than just writers. It's right to take issue with this double standard. Why should women's fiction be a category if there is no male equivalent? But this conversation becomes more nuanced outside of fiction, with categories we might not be so keen to scrap—like Women's Studies (which still exists as a BISAC code, though most writers and scholars refer to it more often as Gender Studies), Women in Politics, and Literary Criticism/Women.

My time at Seal Press showed me the value of publishing books for women by women, and in doing this work, the all-female staff were the ones setting the parameters of our readership. And there are authors who set out to write books for women only, as is the case with this book. If someone reviews *Write On, Sisters!* and says it will appeal to women, or if only women's media cover it, I'm okay with that, but that's because it's on my terms. Women fiction authors don't feel the same way, because they're not setting the terms if their publishers are placing their books in women's fiction. And, to further complicate things, women authors who might pull themselves out of women's fiction do so to the detriment of their own books, because it's a category that drives a lot of discoverability and sales.

A second bind of categorization impacts all authors, but perhaps women more than men because women writers tend to defy categorization more often. In her 1983 book, *How to Suppress Women's Writing*, Joanna Russ wrote, "The assignment of genre can function as false categorization, especially when work appears to fall between established genres and can thereby be assigned to either (and then called an imperfect example of it), or chided for belonging to neither." I see this playing out all the time because of the space She Writes Press and SparkPress occupy in the industry. Writers often tell me that they cannot find agents to represent them or publishers who will take a risk on them because their books are both/and, and therefore problematic. A writer may be writing something that's both a romance and a mystery, for instance, or a book that's commercial fiction and a thriller, and the industry doesn't know what to do with these books or these authors. I won't paint such a broad stroke as to suggest that men are better conformists who always stay in their assigned lane, but my lived experience as a publisher of books by women is that a lot of women deal with false categorization and get accused by the industry of having executed imperfect stories.

In a perfect world, no writer would have to deal with the fallout of categorization. It's tough when you have a book that doesn't fit or that crosses boundaries, or to be slapped with a label you don't like. I think back with a tinge of regret on all the women's-issues books Seal Press published. These included an anthology about women's love-hate relationship with cleaning, a book about home buying for women, a polemic about the role of the media in women's lives, and countless others. How would these books have been categorized if men had written them? I don't know, and I never considered it at the time. But I regret how we, as a feminist press, reinforced the idea that "things women care about"— whether we're talking about cleaning house, buying a home, or how media impact our lives—should be relegated to a separate space.

That said, we wanted women to find these books and we live in a culture that insists on categories, sometimes helpful, sometimes necessary, oftentimes frustrating. As a woman who was married to a woman for ten years, is raising a child who has two moms, and dates women, I find that people classify me as a lesbian. Whether I want this label to be a defining thing, or *the* defining thing, about me is inconsequential. People of color and people in the LGBT community know this experience well; they're defined by their race or their sexual orientation or both, for being *other* than white or straight. Straight white women don't have to contend with this type of classification too much in their regular lives, but they do in writing, because, just as white and heteronormative is the dominant paradigm in our culture, in book publishing it's simply white and male. My point is that I could insist I'm just a woman, and I *am* just a woman, but we live in a world where socially enforced differences are an inescapable part of daily life.

To women writers, I say let's fight for our legitimacy where we must and own being category defiers and writers of women's fiction. (Meanwhile, I'll make a personal commitment here on the page to ask the Book Industry Study Group, the association responsible for determining category codes for books, to add men's fiction as a subcategory of fiction.) We can work toward systemic change, but perhaps most important in this conversation is focusing our attention on our readers and looking at our womanhood as the source of strength and power that it is—categories be damned.

Double Standards

In 2007, I edited a book by Jessica Valenti called *He's a Stud, She's a Slut, and 49 Other Double Standards Every Woman Should Know.* Among the double standards in this book are "He's a Hero, She's a Damsel" and "He's a Politician, She's a Fashion Plate." One of the consequences of working on this book was that I started seeing double standards everywhere. Once your eyes are opened to them, they're hard to unsee.

Book publishing's double standards have traditionally been a mirror into privilege. Common double standards I see include the following:

- Women writers have their lives reviewed, while male writers get to have their books reviewed. In a 2018 *Guardian* article, "How to Refocus the Spotlight on Female Writers," Rhiannon Lucy Cosslett wrote, "So much of the criticism of women's writing is explicitly personal—the words on the page aren't always the only thing reviewed—the author's mothering, her sexual experiences, her emotional responses all come under "literary" scrutiny."[2]

- Women memoirists are diarists, while male memoirists are brave. A 2017 review of Roxane Gay's *Hunger* calls her a diarist and takes a rather condescending note in this critique: "It is curious to be reminded . . . that [Gay] was first drawn to online forums by the promise of anonymity. The memoir deals with her rape, her over-eating, and her struggles with her public and private identities." As if the reasons that draw a woman writer to start writing should remain unchanged and static over time. In Cosslett's 2018 *Guardian* article, Joyce Maynard was quoted as saying, "When a male writer exposes raw personal truths (let's take [Karl Ove] Knausgaard, for example), he's simply courageous." Note that Knausgaard's six-part, 3,600-page autobiographical novel (which, as such, I feel comfortable comparing to memoir) was routinely and consistently praised for its artistry and remarkableness, though what makes him a celebrated novelist and Gay a diarist is hard to discern. In a refreshingly honest 2016 Book Riot piece called "On Holding Women Memoirists to an Unfair Higher Standard," Nicole Froio wrote, explaining that she'd been avoiding reading women memoirists, "I was holding women's memoirs (and their authors) to much higher standards than the same genre written by male authors."[3]

- **Women write nuanced, believable male characters, while male writers don't have to extend the same courtesy to their female characters.** It's long been debated whether women write male characters better than men write women, and vice versa. The fact is, many celebrated novels showcase amazing writing on both sides: Gillian Flynn's *Gone Girl*, Jeffrey Eugenides's *The Marriage Plot*, Wally Lamb's *She's Come Undone*, and Donna Tartt's *The Secret History*. This smattering of examples doesn't show a full picture, though, which is women write male characters less often. In a 2013 *Atlantic* article, Sally Koslow, in response to the question of why women don't take on male characters more often, is quoted as saying, "A novel takes two years out of your life, so I am more comfortable living with characters I know." Her sentiment may echo other women's, but it's also the case that women writers are held to a higher standard when it comes to executing male characters, whereas men can get away with absurd characterizations of their female characters. A 2018 *Observer* piece, "Twitter Challenge Proves Male Authors Don't Know How to Write About Women," covered a Twitter challenge from podcaster Whit Reynolds that read:

  > @whitneyarner
  > new twitter challenge: describe yourself like a male author would

Most of the responses are funny, but the point of the challenge was "to showcase how male authors are often dismissive of female characters, a problem that has persisted for decades."[4]

- Women write about an issue and they're writing for women, while men write about a similar issue and they're writing for everyone. There are countless examples here, but parenting comes to mind because it's the kind of topic that when authored by women is for women and when authored by men automatically takes on more significance. Let's take the case study of Po Bronson's 2009 *NurtureShock* and its heavy-hitting subtitle, *New Thinking About Children*. Yes, Bronson's coauthor, Ashley Merryman, is a woman, but the reviews of this book and Bronson's name recognition and position as lead author indicate that the industry treated this as a male-authored book. Let's compare it with a similarly researched and scientifically driven book, Angela Garbes's 2018 *Like a Mother: A Feminist Journey Through the Science and Culture of Pregnancy*. This is an imperfect comparison, because I realize that Bronson's book is about child rearing (ostensibly for everyone) and Garbes's book is about pregnancy (meaning it's likely to appeal to a women-exclusive audience, though it shouldn't). Still, my hope was to address how publishers position books, one to be for everyone and the other to be for women. Let's start with the covers: *NurtureShock* has a gray-white background. Its central image is a big, cracking egg held together by a Band-Aid. *Like a Mother* has a pale pink cover featuring a silhouette of a very pregnant woman and lines shooting outward from the woman's body in every direction, suggesting a vague reference to Wonder Woman. *NurtureShock* is categorized in Social Sciences and Psychology, while *Like a Mother* is categorized in Women's Health and Motherhood. Not surprisingly, *NurtureShock* was infinitely more widely reviewed—by the *Washington Post*, the *New York Times*, *Library Journal*, and even the *Financial Times* (which seems an unlikely outlet to cover a woman's book about pregnancy and childbirth), while the best publicity *Like a Mother* has gotten to date is *Fresh Air*. Both books got *Publishers Weekly* reviews, in which *NurtureShock* was called "provocative" but also dinged for its "chatty reportage" and *Like a Mother* was lauded for how well the author addressed the biology of pregnancy and for her "introspection."

- Women who submit get penalized for their gender, while men who submit get the green light. In a 2015 Jezebel article, Catherine Nichols wrote about what she learned from sending out her novel under a male name—namely, that she got many more responses from agents when she submitted as such. Nichols contacted some fifty agents using her real name and heard back from only two. When she changed gender, however, she received responses from five out of six agents, including three manuscript requests.[5]

    "He is eight and a half times better than me at writing the same book," she wrote. "Fully a third of the agents who saw his query wanted to see more, where my numbers never did shift from one in 25."

A 2016 Bustle article, "Gender Bias in Publishing Is Real—and This Study Proves It," cited two separate studies, one American (The VIDA Count) and one Australian (The Stella Count), which showed basically the same thing, that:

> "two-thirds of published authors in Australia are women, [but] two-thirds of the books being reviewed are by men—a ratio that has remained largely the same for 30 years." The 2014 Stella Count, which analyzes review trends in Australian publications, found that, out of all of the twelve newspapers it examined, "the proportion of reviews by men of female authors was less than 17 percent." In the United States, the 2014 VIDA Count showed similarly abysmal numbers, particularly where books by women of color were concerned.

VIDA, an organization committed to creating transparency about the lack of gender parity in the literary landscape, per its website, does an annual byline count to "highlight gender imbalances in publishing by tallying genre, book reviewers, books reviewed, and journalistic bylines." The most recent VIDA Count numbers available at the time of this writing were from 2017. The results show that we still have a ways to go in book publishing, as in journalism: "Unfortunately," VIDA's observation report read, "the undeniable majority, 8 out of 15 publications, failed to publish enough women writers to make up even 40% of their publication's run in 2017."

The publishing industry is not doing enough to confront double standards, but only in recent years has there been a real demand for change, as opposed to just grousing that these things are true, followed by a collective throwing-up of hands. Today's environment for holding publishers accountable is decidedly different because of the Internet and social media. Ordinary citizens can demand accountability, and all of us can participate in effecting change by supporting organizations like VIDA and the Op-Ed Project, which both focus on parity within the broader publishing industry (journals, magazines, and newspapers, in addition to books).

The Gender of Genre

The author of a 2016 academic study, "Book Genre and Author Gender," attempting to quantify how many women versus men write in specific genres, wrote, "The overall trend seems to be for females to be the majority in life-focused subjects, from life sciences to the arts and humanities, whereas males dominate in the rest. A simplistic characterization of this might be that women have more interest in human relationships and nurturing whereas males tend to be more interested in making things. The reasons for imbalances are complex, however."[6]

Yes, the reasons men dominate in all but life-focused subjects are complex, but I also think we can say what's true here, which is that women are pushed to the margins. Girls and women are also *directed* toward pursuing interests having to do with human relationships and nurturing, whereas boys and men are *directed* toward interest in making things. In the newsroom, women journalists are often relegated to human-interest stories. The newsroom is notorious for being patriarchal via making excuses about concern for women's security, that women aren't strong enough to handle field assignments, that women will face violence. All of these things may be true, but for concerns that men do not face to direct what women are allowed to do is the very definition of gendered socialization, if not discrimination.

To punctuate my point, a 2014 *Washington Post* article noted that reporters for the ten major American newspapers were 62.2 percent male, versus 37.8 female, and that the number of female bylines was far fewer than those of their male counterparts. (The *New York Times* was the worst offender, with 31 percent female bylines.)

That women journalists are prevented from taking the assignments they want or steered toward softer issues parallels the publishing industry, of course. Women authors have higher barriers to overcome to prove their authority. I've heard countless stories of women authors whose books were rejected because publishers said they didn't have the necessary credentials or authority. Or they're rejected because of the publisher's estimation that there's not a big enough audience for their work. We'll never know how many women-authored books have been written and not published because authors couldn't secure a publishing deal for any one of these reasons or others.

Let's look at Figure 1, which is from the abovementioned study, "Book Genre and Author Gender," and charts a few interesting trends about authorship—namely, that women publish more fiction than men. This seeming gain would be noteworthy were it not for the massive gender

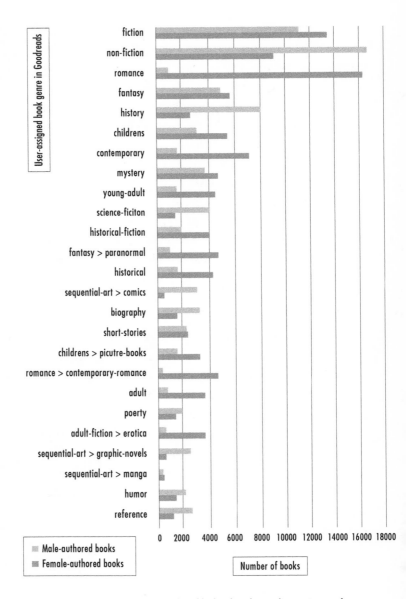

FIGURE 1: The number of books by male and by female authors in the top 25 genres from the crawled sample. [Color figure can be viewed at wileyonlinelibrary.com]

inequities where reviews and awards are concerned, as well as for those titles that top best-seller lists. The study's authors noted that of the books that topped the *New York Times* adult fiction best-seller list from 1960 to 2015, 37 percent were written by women authors, in comparison with 56 percent by men authors. (We'll dive deeper into who wins awards a little further on in this chapter.)

The vast disparities between female and male authors when it comes to nonfiction and romance is analogous there being fewer women in the sciences and fewer men becoming elementary school teachers. It shows how, culturally, men and women gravitate more to certain realms—whether in careers or genres—based on cultural expectations, or one might argue, conditioning. Romance may well be a genre for women by women—with female protagonists and too-hot men or beautiful couples embracing often featured on the covers—but this article speculated that that the "historical association of romance with femininity may repel many men." *Repel.* What we have here is an academic article identifying how misogyny shows up in reading preferences. Romance may target women, but since nonfiction doesn't suffer from similar gender constraints, the fact that so many more male authors pen nonfiction reiterates my earlier argument that women's writing is for women, while men's writing is for everyone.

The next chart, Figure 2, shows a picture of specific genres authored by men and women, and here we see a wholly different picture, in which women strongly dominate the romance and historical fiction genres (and somewhat dominate animals, memoir, and fantasy) while men dominate everything else.

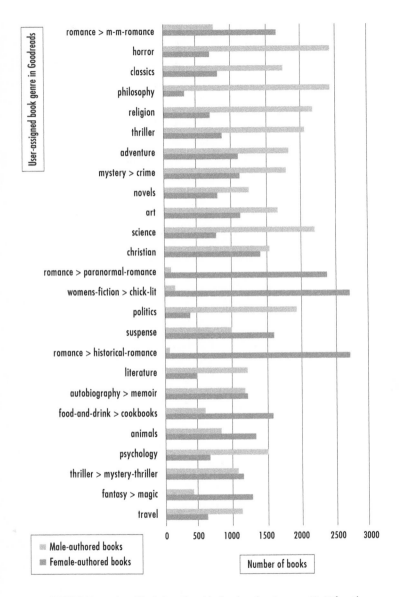

FIGURE 2: The number of books by male and by female authors in genres 26–50 from the crawled sample. [Color figure can be viewed at wileyonlinelibrary.com]

This study concluded that there are "unexpected almost universal authorship gender differences" across the genres they studied. For me, this is not at all unexpected. The only unexpected finding reported was that there was no clear gender-based relationship between authors' success (in terms of how many books they sold) and their prevalence within a genre. This is encouraging because it means that there's a readership for women in whatever genre they choose to write.

We're not even close to gender parity in publishing, but one of the first steps in getting there is to publish. This starts with the belief that your voice matters. Be suspicious of arbitrary rejection, and especially don't wield that rejection against yourself. Instead, use it as a sword to fight the good fight, to see your work through in whatever capacity you can. Chapter 8 of this book is dedicated to how and why to publish your work and how to amplify your voice. For now, make a commitment not to hide the light of your words or put your manuscript in some file buried deep in your computer or in the proverbial drawer. Make a commitment that you'll let it see the light of day.

The Gender Imbalance of Reviews and Awards

Who gets reviewed, and who receives literary awards? Not surprisingly, there's a major gender imbalance here, which shows just how insidious cultural conditioning is and how it negatively impacts women writers.

In 2010, a *New Republic* article titled "The READ: Franzen Fallout" was published in response to novelists Jennifer Weiner and Jodi Picoult calling the *New York Times* Book Review a "boys' club." Ruth Franklin, who wrote the article, did some digging into the authors' claims and discovered that this wasn't just some spat. Indeed, the *New York Times* really did review more fiction by men than by women—far more. The article stated, "Over about two years, from June 29, 2008 to August 27, 2010, the *Times* reviewed 545 works of fiction—338, or 62 percent, were by men. During that period, 101 books got the 'one-two punch' of a review in both the daily *Times* and the *Sunday Book Review*—72 of them were by men."

A *New Republic* 2011 follow-up piece, entitled "A Literary Glass Ceiling?," also by Franklin, included a response from Peter Stothard, of the *Times Literary Supplement,* when he was called out for similar gender imbalances at his outlet. "The *TLS*," he told the *Guardian,* "is only interested in getting the best reviews of the most important books." In the original *Guardian* article, he added, "Without making a fetish of having 50/50 contributors, we do have a lot of reviewers of both sexes and from all over the world. You have to keep an eye on it but I suspect we have a better story to tell than others."

The unconscious bias Stothard exudes with this comment would almost be laughable if it didn't have such serious consequences for women writers. The very idea that getting to parity would be a "fetish" is patronizing, but women writers have to be able to recognize that words like these are patronizing before we can fight them. Women will be told that their work is simply not as good. We want only the best books, the best reviews, these outlets will say, failing to recognize the inherent bias, fed by cultural conditioning, that exists in male-dominated spaces that favor male writers. Gender imbalances do not exist because women are not as good; they exist because men fear parity. We can't make them feel less threatened, but we certainly can and will refuse to back down.

It won't come as a surprise that awards parallel reviews in their gender imbalance. A 2016 Quartz article said it all with its headline, "Women Are Horribly Under-represented in the World's Top Literary Awards." This article summarized a few facts: "Since 1950, when the US National Book Awards were established, only one quarter of the prizes in its fiction category have gone to women." In addition to the gender gap that exists in the prize winners themselves, there's another one, which is the gender disparity in the winning authors' main characters. "Novels in which the main character is female," Quartz reported, "win far fewer prizes than novels with a male main character."[7]

In 2015, Nicola Griffith wrote a blog post called "Books About Women Don't Win Big Awards," in which she tracked the gender of the author and the protagonist over the preceding fifteen years of prize winners of six major fiction awards: the Pulitzer Prize, the Man Booker Prize, the National Book

(continued on next page)

(continued from previous page)

Award, the National Book Critics Circle Award, the Hugo Award, and the Newbery Medal. The results, in all their pie-chart glory, are pretty staggering. Griffith's simple conclusion: "The literary establishment doesn't like books about women."[8]

The most prestigious awards in book publishing have come under enough public scrutiny for their lack of inclusivity that an entire volume could be filled with the critiques. The *Guardian* ran a piece in January 2018 titled "Women write literary fiction's big hitters. So where are their prizes?" in which it noted that the Man Booker Prize still favors men. The reason it's so important that these contests listen to the criticism they're getting is that women writers' time has come. Confronting a bias requires acknowledging that a bias exists. Understanding what cultural influences are at play is necessary if we are to begin to change the dialogue. And the old boys' club needs to listen in order for women to truly be recognized for the strong work they're doing, rather than being undermined.

Backlash

One of the great privileges of having come of age in the 1980s in a progressive household, the oldest child of two working parents with liberal social ideals, is that I was raised to believe I could become anything I wanted to become. Women Gen Xers, millennials, and Gen Zers who come from families with means largely share this orientation to the world. We are the generations who came after the women's movement, and the most reverberating positive impact of that movement has been how girls are raised. We do believe we can do anything. We know we're as competent and capable as boys. We are not afraid of our strength and intelligence, and in many ways we are coming into our full power as the oldest members of Gen X reach their fifties. Yes, we are a force to be reckoned with.

That said, we still have a long way to go. Women still make eighty cents on the dollar compared with their male counterparts. We still face sexism and gender bias. We're still underrepresented in positions of power. We still don't have full control over our own bodies. We still experience sexual harassment, sexual assault, and sexual violence as a very symptom of being female.

A complicated fact of social change is that it's hard to measure. It can be deceiving, too, because if you're like me and you grew up to believe you could be anything you wanted to be, and you're on your path and you feel as if you have some authority and are exercising your voice, it can seem like nothing is standing in your way. But society will show you otherwise, again and again and again—through policies that negatively impact women, through a collective refusal to right gender disparities, and through behavior that reiterates to women that we are not equal and that our voices matter less. For every two steps forward we take, we take a giant step backward, because whenever women make social progress, we confront backlash.

Susan Faludi's 1991 book, *Backlash: The Undeclared War Against American Women*, documented in 552 pages a media-driven backlash against the feminist advances of the women's movement of the 1970s. She wrote, "The anti-feminist backlash has been set off not by women's achievement of full equality but by the increased possibility that they might win it. It is a pre-emptive strike that stops women long before they reach the finish line."

When I had the great privilege to see Faludi onstage at the 2018 Milford Readers and Writers Festival, and then to speak with her afterward, she told me that *Backlash* could just as easily have been written today. Backlash is the fear that results when those who hold the reins of power realize that they've given too much slack, that the very progress certain classes of people have been pushing for, and especially making gains toward, seem to threaten and upend the powers that be—so they yank on the reins, oftentimes setting in motion policies and laws and even condoning behavior that keeps women (and minorities and immigrants, too, of course) in their place.

The 2016 presidential election was a petri dish experiment in backlash if we ever needed one. It showed us on a national stage what the acceptable range of behavior is for both men and women. People can talk until they're blue in the face about all the ways in which Donald Trump has defied social conventions, and they do, but the fact that he gets away with it, that he sets the tone, and that his behavior has encouraged more openly hostile—and sexist and racist—rhetoric is our fault, not his.

This 2018 tweet from @SoSofieFatale, reflecting upon how the media covered Trump and Hillary Clinton at George H. W. Bush's funeral, captured the profound double standard I'm addressing:

> A man can be an insufferable asshole 364 days a year & the media will suggest on the 1 day he's not that he's turned a positive corner. A

woman can sit still & ignore the man who's spent
two years screaming for her imprisonment & be
called a rude bitch.

In 2014, in response to the fact that people were
picking up *Backlash* for book clubs, Faludi published a
piece on Medium about her journey to get it published—
the fact that it wasn't initially well received (no surprise
there) and that it got a tiny advance (amazing that it got
one at all)—and countering the allegation by some that
she'd written the book as some sort of "prestige move."
Such ridiculous accusations would never be lobbed at
a man. Faludi's book is intellectually rigorous and well
researched, and most authors who write serious cultural
critiques do so because they already have the prestige
(i.e., credentials, gravitas, knowledge) to do so.

"On the upside," Faludi wrote, "as backlash media
messages have donned female-friendly guises, women
have become more sophisticated at seeing through the
masks." Yes, thank goodness. We are savvier at identifying the bullshit as such when it's being slung at us.
In concluding the piece, she wrote, "One of my biggest
worries about our current times is the way in which
pervasive self-congratulation about 'how far we've
come' elevates small successes while obscuring the dire
economic straits of the vast majority of the female population. We compliment ourselves that our era is more
enlightened, more progressive, more inclusive—even as
gains that women thought they'd secured slip away."[9]

Ironic that this was written in 2014. Faludi needn't
have worried. A giant backlash came along in 2016 to
remind anyone who might have been leaning too far into

self-congratulatory territory that if you lean too far too soon, you're going to get whiplash.

What's true of the experience of being a woman is that we have a lot to navigate and a lot to overcome if we want to be heard once we claim our place at the table. So many women writers I work with are afraid to come on too strong. They fear what other people will think of them. They don't trust their own opinions about things; they constantly qualify and apologize too often for nothing. They worry about being "too"—too much, too loud, too opinionated. Women temper their self-expression in an attempt to accommodate and not offend—in effect, to adhere to cultural expectations of what a woman *should* be: accommodating, warm, and congenial; independent but not too independent; smart but not to the extent of outshining; capable but not bossy.

To put your voice out into the world is to both believe and demand that what you have to say matters. We are our best selves when we assert our independence and self-reliance, our strength and toughness. The very qualities our culture values least in women are the ones women need to succeed. Understanding this disparity between what our culture thinks is "ideal" feminine behavior and how we may actually feel or behave is helpful, because we should be under no illusion that our endeavors to write and publish, to make our voices heard, to claim our place at the table, are easy or even welcome. They're not. Which makes the fact that we do these things every single day all the more remarkable.

CHAPTER 3:

A Woman Must Have Money

ew topics are more loaded than money when it comes to publishing and the question of who gets published and why. Let's return to *A Room of One's Own* for a moment to recall its central theme—Virginia Woolf's idea that "a woman must have money and a room of her own if she is to write fiction." For Woolf, the room was more than a room; it was a symbol of economic independence and freedom from the expectations placed on women at the time—to run the home, to raise children, to take care of everyone else's needs ahead of their own.

Ninety years since the publication of Woolf's seminal work, women still need economic independence in order to write, and whose voices get heard and what stories get to be told cannot be wholly separated from means, social standing, and class privilege. I have grappled with these questions for years, ever since 2004, when I started working at Seal Press. I got the dose of feminist theory I missed in college during my early years as an acquiring editor there, as I read about the women's movement and its many gains, as well as missteps. In her book *Feminist Theory*, author and activist bell hooks wrote, "Had poor women set the agenda for the feminist movement, they might have decided that class struggle would be a central feminist issue." She further argued that class oppression wasn't a central focus in women's rights movements because the "values, behaviors, and lifestyles continue to be shaped by privilege."[1]

This idea parallels that of what gets published. It's easy to make the case that book publishing has historically seen the world through a particular set of values, behaviors, and lifestyles that privilege has shaped. Yet this doesn't mean that privileged women shouldn't publish, or that they should somehow take a seat to make room for someone else. In fact, I'll argue exactly the opposite as we explore not only the economics of publishing but also how our self-worth and conditioning play out through a financial lens—messages that our writing isn't worthwhile, that we should somehow be focused on the return on investment of our work, that there should be some limit to what we spend on our hobbies, or that our ambitions are hobbies only until we succeed monetarily. All of these things are in the mix here. Still, in order to move forward with an awareness of our own impact, we must ponder the question of whose stories don't get told. This matters because before the twenty-first century, the answer to this question was, most women's stories. Today those who are left on the margins are almost always women of color and lower-income women, but other oppressions play a role, too. Other oppressions play a role, too. Women might get left out because they're not able to make financial decisions because a partner holds the purse strings, or because they don't feel they're allowed to prioritize their own ambitions over something like a child's college fund or a much-needed family car.

In some cases, hard economic realities exist but can be overcome. I've seen women make excuses, insist that they don't have the money to write, when in fact they're simply not seeing their writing as valuable enough to invest in. I hope this chapter provides an opportunity for any woman writer to sort out what her relationship with money is. To ask, *Do I have and make my own money? Do I get to choose what I spend it on? Do I get to make sole decisions about my money, or do I make these decisions in collaboration with a partner or someone else? Do I think my writing is worth spending money on, or do I believe that if my work were good enough, it would be financially supported in the form of a publishing deal?*

As the publisher of an author-subsidized publishing house, I subsidize my own publishing just like any other author on our list. Though I'm solidly in the middle class, I'm a single mom and I don't have tons of extra money to throw at my publishing endeavors. Each time I publish my own work, I feel the financial squeeze, yet this will be my third single-author book since 2012. I've prioritized publishing my work as an act of self-expression, but also as a means by which to grow my author platform—and thereby my expertise and authority. My books keep me relevant and establish me as a go-to person in my field. This can all be true for novelists and memoirists as well, and it's always the case that your publishing journey will be only as awesome as you determine it will be.

Any conversation about money is likely to be fraught, and I hope to tackle this chapter with the nuance and sensitivity the topic deserves. I understand that marginalized voices are marginalized because of historical inequities. I understand that the very nature of running an author-subsidized press is such that the majority of our authors are women of means. (As an aside, this is why, in 2017, She Writes Press initiated its STEP program—She Writes Press Toward Equality in Publishing—to publish two female writer of color every year, one on She Writes Press and one on SparkPress.) I also understand the luxury that voice and agency are when someone is struggling with subsistence-level needs.

With all these things being true, I also know the financial struggles that some women who publish with She Writes Press face because I talk to prospective authors every day. I hear their angst and their inability to justify the cost and the countless reasons—some legitimate and some excuses—why they can't afford it. *Especially* the women of means. So I ask you to join me in the unfolding of this chapter, which aims to shed some light on women's relationship with money, while understanding that what we're about to explore works on the assumption that most of my readers have the means and/or the agency to write and are entertaining—or, better yet, fully embracing—the prospect of publishing.

Who Gets Paid?

When She Writes Press was getting off the ground, one of the biggest criticisms we faced was our business model, even though we were fully transparent about what we hoped to achieve from the get-go, and even though authors receive higher royalties—60 percent of print sales, as opposed to the 7.5 percent they'd receive were they to publish on a traditional press—in exchange for their investment in their own publishing endeavor. I am not independently wealthy and did not have investors, so giving authors advances was never on the table, nor did I ever entertain the idea that She Writes Press could finance editorial, production, or printing expenses on behalf of its authors.

Paramount to me was that our arrangement was transparent and fair to the authors. The author invests and thereby carries the risk; if the book does well, the author benefits proportionately. Still, criticism was lobbed from various corners of the writing world that I was well immersed in. A colleague I knew who started a different women's writing platform a couple years later told me, "We believe in paying writers." I knew it was a direct attack on our model, but I didn't take the bait. It's not that She Writes Press doesn't believe in paying authors. Our authors don't have to earn out an advance or any expenses, so they start earning back their investment right away. And all around me I was seeing how unsustainable it was to be a small publisher, to take little bets and hope they'd pay off. Those publishers who weren't getting creative were having to sacrifice elsewhere, mostly in the arena of turning down fabulous projects simply because they couldn't make the numbers work.

In order for a publishing house to offer an advance and cover the costs of editorial, production, and printing, the editorial team has to at least feel like it's making a sound bet, which means believing that it will at least earn back its expenses. Countless beautifully written manuscripts that are ready to become books and find their audience do not meet this threshold for publishers.

Consider a book that gets a $10,000 advance. In

order for an author to start making royalties, she will have to not only earn back that $10,000 in sales but also earn back the editorial, production, and printing costs, which can easily total $10,000–$15,000, if not more. A publisher that makes a $25,000 investment, therefore, is looking at its author as a liability, as someone who needs to recoup $25,000 in order for the publisher to break even. Based on retail prices and steep discounts to its accounts, a publisher needs to sell at least five thousand copies to break even on our case-study book. And while this number may not sound like a lot to first-time authors who have their sights set on selling tens of thousands of books, selling five thousand copies of a debut book (heck, any book) is actually quite difficult, and that makes this kind of investment a tough judgment call for any publisher.

Most authors subscribe to the belief that getting paid for their work legitimizes their efforts. I want to offer an alternate way of thinking about legitimization, however, especially because of how broken the traditional publishing industry is, how few debut authors can hope to get a publishing deal these days, and what kinds of sales publishers have to project to justify taking on a new author. No agent or publisher or editor can legitimize your work for you. Only you can. And if you're tying the worthiness of your book to a publisher offering you money for it or subsidizing its publication, a quick history lesson might prove interesting here, because, as it turns out, the very idea that writing *should* earn an author her living is only a couple hundred years old.

At the 2014 Muse and the Marketplace writers' conference, industry expert Jane Friedman delivered a keynote called "Writing for Love (and Money)," in which she gave a fascinating rundown on the history of authorship that I'll paraphrase here, though I encourage readers to watch her full presentation online. In the early days of writing—during the time of the Reformation in the 1500s and earlier—it was not even culturally accepted that writers would get paid to publish. Writers instead saw themselves as conduits and collaborators, as bringing forth a gift to the world, rather than creating something with a stamp of their authorship on it. The very idea that what people wrote might bring them fame or recognition was considered distasteful. In the 1600s and 1700s, things shifted and cults of personalities rose up alongside authors, but, even so, writers were still not paid to publish. People who gravitated toward writing and publishing either were born wealthy or had patrons. The prevailing sentiment among these authors was that the immortalization of their words was enough—meaning, more so than earning any money at writing, fame was their end goal.

In 1710, the first copyright law was passed in England, resulting in the first wave of authors rejecting money from patrons in favor of taking earnings from sales. The rise of the middle class (and with it, literacy) in the late 1700s and 1800s facilitated this shift. With more readers, authors were able to sustain themselves on sales alone. They set a precedent that writers *could* make a living at their writing. More writers ushered in a more thriving publishing industry, and with more avenues to publish, more writers wrote and published. In the early 1900s, the royalty system as we understand it today emerged and authors began getting advances for their work. Soon, rather than an exception, this became the expectation among authors, setting a cultural precedent that those books "worthy" of being published were those that a publisher supported financially.[2]

We can revisit the conversation about gatekeepers in Chapter 2 as a reminder that what gets published has nothing to do with what's best or most worthy, or even with what readers want most. So placing the value of your work at the feet of agents and editors, given how they make their choices, might require a reassessment, just as the entire romanticized ideal of getting paid to publish calls for a reframe. In her "Writing for Love (and Money)" keynote, Friedman talked about the "era of universal authorship," in which everybody is writing *something*, and referenced a quote by George Packer, of the *New Yorker*, who said, "Writing has become one of the higher forms of recreation in a leisure society."

The biggest ramification of so many more voices and so many more writers writing and wanting to publish is that there as many or more writers as there are readers. More books and fewer readers have meant that publishing houses are taking fewer risks. Because there's no shortage of writers willing to write for less or for free, outlets that traditionally paid authors to write are paying less or nothing. The idea of exposure over payment isn't popular in some circles, but so many writers are willing to do it that it's changed how magazines and online content aggregators value (or don't value) writing.

For years I blogged for the *Huffington Post* for free, along with countless other contributors. The reason I did this was to get eyes on my work—and it was absolutely worth it. The exposure my articles got brought authors to She Writes Press and writers to my coaching website.

When my pieces got featured, I got a lot of attention for them on social media. When one post went viral, it was picked up by industry magazines and mentioned in *Forbes* and the *New Republic*. This suddenly made me an influencer, and that kind of reach well offset any money I might have wished to be earning from those posts.

Way beyond blogging, publishing a book gives writers exposure, which explains why authors self-publish or opt to publish on a hybrid press like She Writes Press and others, investing in their work for the visibility it gives them, for the doors it invariably opens, and also, in some cases, simply to make a mark or to fulfill a dream.

It's interesting to note that in some ways authorship has come full circle, having increasingly become something most writers don't expect to be paid to do. And if writing is a form of higher recreation, or, as I know it to be for so many writers, a way to feed their souls, then money takes a backseat. For many writers, money is not the thing that's driving them to write, or to publish for that matter.

Too many people write well, and too many people have stories worth telling. To me, this is a good thing, but its consequences are problematic when it comes to conversations about money. In her 2019 post on Electric Literature titled "The Disastrous Decline in Author Incomes Isn't Just Amazon's Fault," Carrie V. Mullins posited one reason why authors are earning less than ever before: because "discernment has taken a backseat to access,"[3] meaning that people are more likely to read content if it's accessible—and if it's free—than just because it comes from a reputable source. There's good news and bad news for new and emerging authors here.

On the one hand, authors have a fair shot. There's a more level playing field than ever before, and most readers don't care what publisher published your work as long as you have something they want to read. On the other hand, it's a tough reality that readers want to consume free content, Amazon keeps book prices super low (especially e-books), and the cost of producing high-quality books, regardless of format, is more expensive than ever.

Meanwhile, for book publishers trying to navigate this tricky world of free (and arguably undervalued content), discernment is at an all-time high; at issue is the confluence of what publishers think will sell, how readers discover new authors and books, and the fact that publishing is easier than ever but earning money at publishing is harder than ever. More and more authors, as the rise of hybrid publishing and self-publishing indicates, are authorizing themselves—manifesting their dreams and green-lighting their own work. By the time someone gets to this place where they're ready to do that, becoming a best-selling author or making tens of thousands of dollars from their writing is not likely to top the list of reasons why they're forging forward with the publication of their book. A debut author is unlikely to become one of the 2 percent who make a living at writing alone. Most successful career authors are cobbling together a living, doing the work they love, and letting their books supplement their creative efforts.

These entrepreneurial authors are the ones whom She Writes Press has served all along, and I know that our authors' success stems from their hard work and understanding of what a book might actually get them. They realize that a book is just one step toward a larger goal. And while I can't really write this without it seeming like I'm throwing it back in my colleague's face, that other publishing platform didn't survive. Yes, it *believed in paying its authors*, but in practice it couldn't make things work and it folded. Aspiring authors will do much better to stop measuring their worth by how much they might get paid to write and instead focus their intention on content generation, getting published, and finding readers. Doing this will help the rest fall into place.

Women and Worthiness

It won't come as a surprise that measures of self-worth stem directly from what our culture values. You'll recall from Chapter 2 the 2017 Pew study about what we value most in women, and that the number-one trait is physical attractiveness. The number-two quality our culture values in men is financial success. And while that's the seventh-highest-ranked value for women, it is on the list, in the top ten. Anyone who's ever attended a party knows that conversation quickly gravitates toward what people do for work. We might be impressed by what someone does for a living because they have a cool job, or sometimes because we perceive that they make a lot of money. When it comes to measuring worth, the important variables seem to be what someone does, how much they make, how much they achieve, how they look, and who they know. This isn't to say that other things don't matter. It matters that we practice kindness, that we give to charity, that we raise our children well, that we are contributing members of our community. But when we look to see whether we're measuring up, the stick our culture encourages us to use is based more on factors that indicate success and less on things that are considered good or important or meaningful.

It should come as no surprise that this focus on success plays into our publishing journeys. For one, the publishing industry will measure your worth by the same cultural values because publishers want to sell, and that means they're looking for authors who check the right boxes. It matters how you look and who you know. How much you achieve plays directly into how desirable an author you will be, because publishers are looking for authors who are doing the hard work of bringing them a readership.

Since we're talking about measures of self-worth, let's talk about worthiness. Its definitions are telling: the quality of being good enough and the quality of deserving attention or respect. I can't think of two things aspiring authors crave more than to know they're good enough and to feel as if they deserve attention and respect. I also can't think of two more elusive things for aspiring authors, and especially for women.

Brené Brown's June 2010 TEDx talk, "The Power of Vulnerability," is a must-watch for anyone who feels as if I just spoke directly to their biggest fears, because she makes the point that our vulnerability is the key to our beginning to believe that we are good enough, that we are deserving. The biggest struggle we have, she argues, is to believe that we're enough. Ultimately, she concludes, the only things that make us worthy are the choices we make. Among the steps we can take to be vulnerable, which sets us on the path toward believing we are enough, is letting ourselves be deeply seen. Short of being intimate with sexual partners, there are few ways in which we're seen as deeply as we are when we write and put our writing out into the world for other people to consume. It's highly vulnerable, which is why it triggers so many intense feelings. Still, according to Brené, that's a good thing, because the act of allowing ourselves to be vulnerable in this way is the very thing that allows us to believe we're good enough and deserving enough. So it's a self-propagating cycle that starts with our risking, and involves our feeling shame, anxiety, and insecurity along the way, and then results in our emerging into a place of feeling more deserving.

Now let's circle back to money, because how much we have is intrinsically tied to our worth—both as the outside world perceives it and as we ourselves see it. We've been talking about worth as synonymous with our values, or our cultural values, but the first definition of worth is monetary value, so it does all in fact come back to money. And the publishing journey, by extension, is all about money, too. You cannot publish and not think about money, whether it's how much you might get for an advance or how much you might spend if you publish independently.

I mentioned that I talk to women about money a lot, and I do. It's on the table in every negotiation I have, and I'm grateful that the women I talk to don't hold back. Sometimes they fret about or bemoan the fact that their publishing journey might have to involve their paying. On the other end of the spectrum, I talk with women who feel empowered by it. Some women decide not to publish because of the cost barrier, while others are ashamed by the very notion that they are considering paying because their conceptions about legitimacy are tied to being accepted by a traditional publisher. I talk with women whose husbands won't let them spend the money, who tell me they can't do it because they have bills to pay, kids to feed. I talk to women who want badly to publish, but they can't, they won't, they don't like the idea of it, and much more.

Here's the deal: It can be expensive to finance your own book, yes. But, as I mentioned earlier in this chapter, for some women the financial impossibility has more to do with conditioning than with reality. I have spoken to women who lambast themselves with judgments that sound very much like they come from the mouths of parents, of partners, of friends. "How can you spend that much on publishing a book?" "Aren't you supposed to get paid to write?" "What if you don't earn back your investment?" The list of questions can go on and on, but I can hear in their tone when they're presented as judgments. I sometimes even hear a tone of accusation toward me as the publisher, as if our company exists solely to make women pay to publish their work.

Of all the women who've told me they legitimately cannot, I've believed them, even if sometimes they've come back later, having implemented the discipline to squirrel away money here and there, or having changed their perspective or having had a change of heart. Sometimes they come back and inform me that they had a heart-to-heart with their husband, and now that they've cleared the air and come clean, they have the support they need to move ahead.

One of my She Writes Press authors, Tammy Hetrick, struggled to justify her publishing expenses at first, in part because her husband couldn't understand why she would spend "so much money" on an endeavor with little chance of making money. She was already nervous about the whole thing, and he was just reinforcing her doubts. But then he turned fifty and bought himself a Ducati motorcycle, with no expectation of any return on investment (ROI), and suddenly she saw spending money on her book project as a perfect analogy: Her novel, *Stella Rose*, was her Ducati. When I asked her to retell this anecdote for this book, she wrote to me in an email:

> It was the biggest toy on my bucket list. It was a lifelong dream come true, a chance to be who and what I always wanted to be. This wasn't about an ROI, as nearly everything else in our lives was. This was about filling my soul with the joy of sharing my creation, like the Ducati filled his soul with the freedom of flying down the road on a masterful machine. I could see the lightbulb switch on for him. His eyes widened, he smiled and said, "I get it," and we never argued about it again.

I once read a poignant novel in progress about a woman who puts $5 per week in a tin box buried in her backyard. In this story, after five years of saving, she suspects her husband has stolen the money to fund his drinking habit, and in one scene she frantically digs up the box to discover that all her money is gone.

Real people can save money this way, and they do. Even lower-income people can put $5 or $10 a week toward their dream. If you saved $5 a week, it would take four years to get to $1,000. If you saved $10 a week, it would take only two years to get there. (Just make sure no one untrustworthy knows where you're stashing your cash.) And you can absolutely publish a book for $1,000. I won't pretend that all the options out there are affordable. Yes, cost barriers exist, but if a writer decides that she matters, if she's in a position where she at least has a choice, then she can save and she can get her words out into the world. My experience is that the money isn't so much what holds women back; more often, it's that they struggle to justify that what they're doing is worthy enough of those hard-earned funds.

Worth is a fraught topic, whether we're talking about it from the standpoint of being good or deserving enough or from the standpoint of whether we're willing to invest in ourselves and our dreams. Historically, women have had less financial agency than men, and that conditioning starts to emerge in the myriad ways in which we buy into the idea that our work doesn't merit investing in, that it's just a hobby, and even that we don't have choices, when in fact we might.

Take a look at your mindset about money. Do some thinking or journaling about what comes up for you when you say the words "My writing is good. My writing is deserving. My writing is worthy of spending money on." It may take some time before you begin to believe that these statements are true, or you might experience the paradox of sometimes believing them things to be true even while you struggle with shame and fear and insecurity. That's okay. It can all be true.

Over coffee in 2018, one of my colleagues shared an experience she had with a group of women writers who were deciding together whether they would invest in a writing retreat for themselves, at the cost of $300 apiece. At some point, one of the women said, "Can you imagine a group of men sitting around and weighing the pros and cons of this like we are?" Her point was that men would have just made the decision. They would have spent the $300 apiece on an experience that was specifically about self-betterment and about pursuing something they wanted, something for them and for their careers. Women can start to do this better. We can start to say yes to ourselves in more overt and decisive ways. We can notice our priorities and begin to see the degree to which we might blindly or unconsciously sacrifice. And then we can stop. We can make small efforts to say yes to ourselves until we get into a pattern of saying yes to as many things as we can that support the belief that we are worth it. We are deserving. We don't have to apologize or feel bad for believing that our creative endeavors matter enough to us that we're going to support them, spend money on them, and champion them with our time, effort, and resources.

Publishing Profits and Price Points

The business of book publishing is complicated even to those who've been in the industry for decades. Parts of it don't make good business sense—like high advances and low retail prices. The way publishing is done stems from the way publishing has always been done. It's an archaic business that's slow to catch up with the times, an industry whose innovators tend to be on the margins while the insiders get swept along with changes they're not controlling, oftentimes much to their chagrin.

The advance is one of those legacy publishing concepts that separates traditional publishing from everyone else, but that doesn't make good business sense as a practice. There's no question that advances are seductive. Even though they're elusive, most aspiring authors still want one, and, as I mentioned above, it's not only for the money but also because an advance equals a financial vote of confidence. The problem is that votes of confidence have zero insurance attached to them, and advances have taken on a strange life of their own in the 2010s, as the Big Five publishers have decided to throw down six- and seven-figure deals in order to secure certain celebrity authors for their lists. The entire process—which involves auctions and bidding wars and culminates in giant advances—runs on high adrenaline and makes book publishers look a whole lot like problem gamblers hitting the Vegas strip.

One editor, quoted in a 2014 *Publishers Weekly* article titled "The Rise of the Seven-Figure Advance," in attempting to explain the enormous advances being bestowed upon the already famous, said, "The whole pool of talent is shrinking. There are fewer publishers, fewer slots, and fewer submissions, so . . . the higher the quality of the project, the more you're likely to get."

But the talent pool is not shrinking. Far from it. It's just that there are fewer "sure bets": the debut (often young and attractive) literary ingenues and celebrities. Publishers cry poor and then throw a million dollars on red. This way of thinking, however, exemplifies my point about the lack of innovation and the sentiment on the part of legacy publishing houses that the best way forward is to acquire celebrities and give them tons of money. In my opinion, this approach is bad for individual publishers and the industry alike because it drives myopic thinking and narrows publishers' choices down to those "sure bets," whatever those might be.

There's no question that for most authors it's decidedly less glamorous to have to pony up the money to publish than it is to get an advance. But if an advance isn't even on the table and might never be, aspiring authors need to start considering what will come next. There are not and have never been sure bets in book publishing. It's a creative industry, and therefore, thankfully, many of the books that rise to the top defy reason and expectation. Thus, what matters most to any author should be the quality of the work they're putting out, the mechanisms by which any publishing solution they might consider can get their book out into the world, and having a handle on who their readership might be and then trying to reach those people.

And then there's what we charge those readers. The truth of book publishing is that authors and publishers alike give readers a great deal on books. Consider this small sampling of book prices (of randomly chosen best-selling hardcovers in their respective years), versus movie prices over the past twenty-five years:

1991: *Scarlett*, by Alexandra Ripley, retailed for $24.95, and the average movie ticket sold for $4.21.

2001: *The No Spin Zone*, by Bill O'Reilly, retailed for $24.95, and the average movie ticket sold for $5.95.

2018: *Less*, by Andrew Sean Greer, retailed
for $26.00, and the average movie ticket sold
for $9.10.

Book prices have remained relatively constant over
twenty-five years, whereas movie prices have doubled. I
feel this when I go to the box office, and while I may not
wish to pay more, the world around us is getting more
expensive. Yet book prices remain constant. Whether
we realize it or not, readers are complicit in undervaluing what a book is worth because of our expectations
about what we're willing to pay. Amazon, with its steep
discounts, supports, even drives, I'd argue, this trend,
and publishers facing the great challenge of making their
books discoverable in a sea of competition acquiesce to it.

In "What Is the Business of Literature?," industry
expert and former Soft Skull Press publisher Richard
Nash, speculating about the value of a book, wondered
why it can be obtained for the cost of a T-shirt. "One
theory from the creative industries," he wrote, "has
been to educate the public that content is worth something, and therefore they should pay for it. That notion
is everywhere, in trailers before movie screenings and in
the pages of magazines, whether they talk about themselves or the book business. As charitable as Americans
are, and as willing as Europeans are to subsidize, relying
on the notion that one deserves to get paid will fail every
time. Imagine that as a dating strategy: I deserve to be
desired by you. Apple, Prada, the NFL, the purveyors of
widely desired goods and experiences do not 'educate'
the public that they deserve to be paid. The public simply
offers up its money, gratefully. The public will not do so

for a basic delivery of a straightforward long-form text experience. If we cannot educate or guilt-trip our way to solvency, then what are we to do?"[4]

These are valid points for consideration by authors and publishers alike. Still, publishers and authors, in response to competition, tend to want to underprice their books. When She Writes Press author Keturah Kendrick got the page proofs for her book, *No Thanks*, she immediately emailed me to ask if we should lower the price. We'd priced her book at $16.95, and when she saw that it was just 188 pages, she asked me, "Should we price it at $13.95?"

My response to her was that we would not charge $13.95, not only because it would be underpricing her book but also because she could potentially lose money on every sale. "We need to charge enough for you to actually make a few dollars on each book," I wrote to her. "So that's the rationale. We could go as low as $15.95, since your book is on the short side, but I wouldn't want to go lower than that."

Her response was swift: "That was just generic fear talking. You're right. I will keep it at $16.95 and trust that it's worth it."

Hell yes, you're worth it, and we also need to educate ourselves and others as readers that authors and books are worth what we pay. As Richard put it in his article, "If it turns out we are not wasting our time and do get a wonderful experience, we get it for $1–$2 an hour, an order of magnitude cheaper than film, theatre, live music, recorded music, dance, a bar, a restaurant, a museum."

There are 101 places where we can and will get tripped up about our worth as authors—from whether we'll pay to publish to how we choose to feel about our self-subsidized projects once they're out in the world to how we want to price our books. If and when you start to get triggered about money, earnings, ROI, price points, or anything else that touches upon finances, stop and go back to those initial questions about money. Do you make your own? Do you have agency? Can you talk to your partner about money? Do you question the worth of what you're doing? You can start to make inroads toward understanding how money and finances are intertwined with your publishing expectations, and therefore your publishing journey, by talking aloud about it, by practicing having uncomfortable conversations, by examining whether you have any judgments about how your work gets out into the world.

You must unpack both the way you feel about money and the way you feel about how worthwhile your writing is in order to have a publishing experience you'll feel good about. Even if you're not in a position to pay for your work, the likelihood that you'll spend something—for publicity, for travel to events, for conferences, for continuing education, for the ongoing opportunity costs that are required to keep yourself in the game—merits examination, which will help you know where you'll land when it's time to decide whether to spend money on yourself.

Sorting out these questions sooner, before the angst of decision making is upon you, will allow you to move forward with confidence, grace, and the ability to say no those expenses you don't think you can justify and yes to the ones you can. This is agency at work, and I know few women who wouldn't benefit from some self-analysis about what they say yes and no to and why. It's hard work, but the outcome is a more confident, self-pos-sessed writer making her way through a self-empowered publishing experience.

Confronting what holds you back is always uncom-fortable, and these financial considerations will be as uncomfortable an issue as any you'll face on your pub-lishing journey. Our feelings about money are deeply ingrained. It can take some serious self-talk to break any feelings you might have about your worth as an artist, or your book's worthiness as something you spend any, let alone a lot of, money on. Know that you're not alone in your reservations. Consider talking about those reserva-tions with others. Bring the fears—which mask feelings of shortcomings, self-doubt, and even shame—into the light. The more you talk about what plagues your worried mind, the more you can sort out what's true and what are just deeply embedded patterns from your upbringing, from society, not yours to carry. Yes, it may turn out that you can't or won't spend money on your creative endeavors, but at least separate out the expec-tations others place upon you from what's true in your heart. Know the difference for yourself between *I can't* and *I won't*, and you'll be better equipped to navigate the possibilities that lie ahead.

CHAPTER 4:

Psychological Warfare

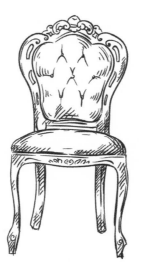

Very few writing classes prepare you for the fact that wielding pen to page or fingers to keyboard is akin to poking a hornet's nest, which when prodded too hard will rouse a beast that lives inside us. The beast goes by many names—the inner critic, the saboteur, the super-ego, the inner mean girl—and some of you may have more than one beast caged up. A writer's inner critic is both common and unoriginal when it comes down to it. Every writer has to grapple with it in some form or another, and its old, worn message is pretty predictable, which can sometimes offer a measure of relief when you realize that the crap you've been telling yourself for years isn't really your crap at all, but widespread among writers everywhere.

I encourage my clients and students to name their inner critic—whether it's an it, a he, or a she. One of my clients calls hers Mazy. Mazy is a heavyset, clunky presence. Everything my client writes is bad in Mazy's eyes, and, as far as Mazy's concerned, my client will never live up to all of the much more inspired and talented novelists who have already published much better books. Mazy would prefer that my client stop her endeavor to write her novel and call it a day. My client has had to work very hard to understand that Mazy is invested in maintaining the status quo and nothing more. Ultimately, Mazy is protecting my client from what Mazy perceives to be inevitable hurt. The problem, of course, is that this comes at the expense of my client's creative process.

One of my memoir students' inner critics is a sticky one. She calls it Gum because that's exactly what it feels like—gummy and hard to get rid of. Gum can't understand why my student wants to air her dirty laundry and would much prefer that she just keep all that personal stuff to herself. Gum is also very into shaming and makes my student feel like there's something wrong with her for wanting to pursue writing her story in the first place. Gum berates her for the fact that she's been working on her memoir for five years now, and seems to take perverse pleasure in reminding her how long it's taking every time my student sits down to write, leaving my student despairing and feeling as if she's no good.

This book so far has been an exploration of the ways in which we are conditioned, and our individual psychologies are at the frontlines of this conversation. All of the historical, social, and economic conditioning that I've addressed so far plays into how we think, feel, and act. This chapter, about emotional conditioning, is the linchpin—the culmination of all of it, and then some—because emotional conditioning comes from all the other conditioning. It comes from our parents and our teachers, our leaders and our mentors.

Addressing emotional conditioning is a big deal because it can start to help us question why we behave the way we do. It asks us to take a look at our belief systems and how they affect our day-to-day lives. When it comes to our writing, emotional conditioning is likely to be the hardest of all the "conditions" to get over, because it's part of who we are. The inner critic is a belief system. Talking about our inner critics is just a way to apply language to our negative beliefs about ourselves. Having an inner critic is part of the human experience, but there's a particular way in which writing, and especially the intention to publish that writing, amplifies the critic's message.

The inner critic is an equal-opportunity offender. Male writers suffer at the hand of their inner critic in the same ways women do. That said, in my experience, women writers experience a unique compounding of conditioning—the historical, cultural, and social conditioning we've been talking about so far in this book, all of which contributes to emotional conditioning like another layer of paint on the canvas of our psyches.

In this chapter, we'll explore emotional conditioning through the lens of the inner critic, and how outer critics (real people in our lives) serve to reinforce those messages. When layered on top of all the other conditioning, these messages can be quite debilitating. Because the inner critic's messages are deeply embedded in our emotional conditioning, many writers have trouble identifying their messages for what they are: ways to hold us back. Recognizing these messages as such and acknowledging who put these ideas into your head in the first place is a good step toward disentangling yourself from your critic's stronghold on your creative process.

Your Insidious and Predictable Inner Critic

In my memoir classes, I've noticed that writers are often soothed to discover that other writers' inner critics sound similar to their own. *You're not good enough. Why are you bothering? Who's going to read this? Who cares about your story?* These are some of the most common messages writers hear. Sometimes the very fact of the inner critic's complete lack of originality can be deactivating for writers. It's like, *Oh, right. There's that familiar put-down, and this entire class of fourteen relates.*

Recognizing an inner critic for what it really is will start to disarm it. It's easier to forge ahead when you realize who your enemy is. But it's even better if and when you can try to understand its purpose and even befriend it. After all, your inner critic is a part of you. There's no process by which you can surgically remove it or become so enlightened that you will it away. The only option you have is to uncover where it came from, better know its motivations, and then work with it.

My mom, a therapist who's done years of her own therapy, is one of the most grounded people I know. In recent years, she's started to write poetry and share it. I've experienced her pride as she's recounted stories of reading her poetry in groups and in one-on-one exchanges with friends and colleagues. But then she published a book of her poems, *Weaving Myself Awake*, and suddenly her inner critic, who had apparently been dormant through all these more intimate sharings, awoke in full onslaught mode and caused my mom to start qualifying these poems she'd previously been so proud of. She began telling men, for instance, that male and/or Christian readers wouldn't relate to or might not like her poems because many of them referenced goddesses. She didn't even realize that she was apologizing for her work until a male friend of hers brought to her attention what she was doing. When he said to her, "I love your poems," it clicked that she was keeping herself too small, thinking her work could be for only a certain kind of readership: women and spiritual seekers.

Inherent in her "you probably won't like this because . . ." talk was her inner critic telling her she wasn't enough. Her poems weren't enough to appeal to a wide audience. Her words weren't enough. *She* wasn't enough. In fact, the poems have touched all kinds of people (men and Christians included!), and the experience of being able to fully own the ways in which her work was touching others created an opening for her to in turn own that she was, indeed, enough. Her poems were enough. Her words were enough. She was enough.

Many writers will have a similar experience—of publishing and receiving positive reinforcement from the outside world. This is wonderful because it serves to counteract the messages that the inner critic, always in replay mode, wants us to hear. While you're still writing, however, getting this kind of positive input can be tough, because unless you're sharing your work with a supportive writing group or receiving some sort of outside validation that's meaningful to you, you are in fact isolated—and your inner critic may well be the loudest voice in the room.

Later in this chapter, I'll cover outer critics, but one piece of advice my coteacher, Linda Joy Myers, and I give students in our memoir classes is not to put the "publishing horse" before the "writing cart." You're likely to experience some outside criticism when you decide to publish, even if it's just a negative review. But in my experience, even those who receive negative feedback about their writing also get a heavy dose of positivity. Regardless, it's best to start to bolster yourself early on.

"I'm Sorry"

Do you notice that you say sorry for no reason? I hear women saying "I'm sorry" when they brush past someone on the street, for inadvertently being in the way, for any old thing, honestly. But what's particularly problematic is saying sorry for speaking, sorry for taking up too much time, too much space. People who *actually* take up too much time and too much space, you see, never apologize for it.

It's okay to be sorry for certain things, of course, like being late, not submitting an assignment, snapping at someone you love, and so on. But women are sorry for things they cannot control. Writers I work with apologize for not remembering something in strong detail, which makes for challenging scene writing, or because their writing isn't good enough when they share after a freewrite. In my coaching practice, women apologize for crying in sessions, having bought into the emotional conditioning message that crying is weak or somehow unseemly.

Qualifying is another form of apologizing. When we qualify, we say things like, "I don't think you're going to like my work." Qualifying is a way of getting out in front of and ultimately protecting ourselves from criticism. The problem is that it also undermines us and our writing. It's important to start noticing whether and how you qualify. You can always add "I'm afraid" to the front of the sentence, too, to see if it rings true. For instance, "I'm afraid you aren't going to like my work" might translate into "I'm afraid that people aren't going to like my work."

Women are expert qualifiers. I qualify my expertise when people ask, "Do you write?" by responding, "Yes, but . . ." On countless occasions, I have responded in this way: "Yes, but I only write books about writing and publishing." I've been consciously attempting to stop this habit. My better answer is, "Yes, I do," or "Yes, I'm the author of several books about writing and publishing."

I'd love to live in a world where women apologize only for things that merit an apology. "Sorry" has become a stand-in for "excuse me," and if you listen, you'll hear that women say it much more than men. Let's level the playing field and choose our words carefully. If you mean excuse me, say excuse me, and watch out for qualifying in your writing and in your life. Hone your confidence muscles by practicing positive statements like "I hope you'll like my work" or "I'm very proud of my writing." The way you talk about your writing will actually change your relationship with it. Practice and see!

Self-Limiting Beliefs

The inner critic is all about limitations. It wants to control you, straitjacket you, squash your creativity, and most definitely prevent you from publishing your work. I mentioned above that some people find it soothing to hear other people share their self-limiting beliefs, so let's break down what those beliefs are to see if you recognize one or all of them in yourself. There is absolutely nothing wrong with you for harboring any of these. I'm not promising any kind of magic bullet to make these messages go away, even in the short term, but sometimes being able to laugh at the inner critic for its absurdity is a good thing. Our goal is to take the bullhorn away from your inner critic and give it a much less prominent role, one of quiet background noise, if not occasional silence.

Message #1: You're not good enough/Who's going to want to read this?

With this message, your inner critic is kicking you where it hurts—tapping into the very thing that matters most to you and trying to shut it down. If it can convince you that you're not as talented as other writers or that your little story doesn't matter, then it's succeeding in making you feel small and unworthy. We feel small and unworthy when we're not seen; when the things that matter most to us are dismissed or, worse, unacknowledged or even delegitimized; when people don't believe us or tell us we're being hysterical. Women experience this kind of emotional manipulation and abuse in spades. Many writers I work with have had parents and other family members show them in many ways that what matters most to them is garbage. If you're a writer who was told as a child that your writing wouldn't amount to anything, or who was criticized for always having your head in the clouds, or who was the family scapegoat, the sensitive one, the black sheep, etc., then this message will undoubtedly resonate with you.

Message #2: Who do you think you are?

This message has a formal name: impostor syndrome. *You're a fake. You're too big for your britches.* The underlying feeling associated with this message is shame. You should be ashamed of yourself for wanting to be recognized. You should be ashamed of yourself for wanting to share your story, for thinking you're important, for believing that what you have to say matters. Sometimes the very thing we long to expose with our writing is something we've been taught to feel ashamed about— and so, through our writing, we trigger more shame.

Do girls experience shaming more frequently than boys? I believe they do. So often, as girls, we are wrong for being female—for how we appeal to boys and men, for how they don't know what to do with us, or for how we make them feel about themselves. So if we try to be seen or acknowledged for the things about us that are bigger and more important than the limiting and confining ideas we have about what women can and should be, then guess what? We're too big for our britches. This is the same as bragging, thinking we're all that. And most women I know have been told that's unseemly. Don't do it. Don't you dare step into the entirety of who you are—because how threatening would that be?

Message #3: Why bother?

Implicit in "Why bother?" is resignation. The inner critic wants you to give up. You have other, more important things to focus your attention on. The question of whether writing is worth the time and effort in the first place won't necessarily resonate with every writer. I work with plenty of writers who live and breathe their writing.

It's become a practice and part of their identity. But for plenty of others, this question of whether the writing is "worthwhile" comes up in all sorts of ways. Sometimes it's about money. *If my writing isn't making me money, why am I pursuing it?* Sometimes it's about recognition or getting work published. *If I haven't gotten anything in print, why am I doing this?* Lots of times it's about what writers think they should have done by a certain point in their lives. I hear some saying, *I'm sixty-five years old, and I'm starting too late. Why bother?* Resignation looks a lot like the Eeyore character in Winnie the Pooh. Eeyore has a woe-is-me outlook on the world. It doesn't take much for him to feel bad about things. *Why bother?* is a symptom of overwhelm and fear of what it's going to take to accomplish your goals. If this message feels true to you, two things: You're not alone, and you just need a little extra encouragement, and perhaps a reminder of why you're doing this in the first place.

Yes, That's Actually Your Inner Critic

It's pretty common for writers not to see the ways in which their inner critics act up and out in their everyday lives. A lot of people are so enmeshed with their inner critics that personality traits and behaviors that actually belong to the critic are fully adapted and integrated and may need to be teased out, which can take time and effort. The following list includes the myriad ways in which writers let their inner critics take over, too often unconsciously. If any of these feels like something you do, again, take heart. They're common patterns, or they wouldn't be on the list. Most of these things we do are crutches we've adopted, often in early life as survival mechanisms. The work of growing our self-confidence and refusing to cultivate self-limiting beliefs lies in letting go of these negative ways of being in relationship with our creativity.

Writers who need excessive reassurance: In these cases, you may be asking the same thing over and over again, not realizing you're fishing for something—a sign that everything is going to be okay; a concrete answer about something that might not be someone else's to give you; a compliment. This behavior has a clinginess to it and is hard to satiate, in part because this kind of writer worries that things are not okay and that they're not okay. For these people, I suggest meditation, because this behavior comes from anxiety. Calming the body calms the mind.

Writers who have a hard time owning how good they are: Women I work with who exhibit this behavior are so self-critical. Oftentimes their work is amazing but they're self-disparaging. These writers can never be good enough, and it's almost impossible for them to see themselves as talented, or good writers. This behavior is connected to impostor syndrome and to a perpetual fear that you're not really deserving, or that you've somehow manipulated your way through this whole creative endeavor of writing and publishing. Practicing giving yourself compliments or doing affirmations is a good way to counteract this tendency.

Writers who can't take a compliment: Here, your inner critic is forcing you to qualify, because you've somehow adopted the belief that accepting a compliment means you're bragging. Nothing could be further from the truth. Graciously accepting a compliment is a reciprocal compliment to the person who gave it to you. This exchange is one that needs to be completed in order for it to be meaningful. If you counter a compliment by shirking it, explaining it, qualifying it, or denying it, you in fact kill this otherwise beautiful human interaction and allow your inner critic to wear away at your self-confidence.

Writers who believe other writers are better, or who fly into panic mode if they find another book that's similar to their book: This behavior stems from a scarcity mentality—that there is only one way to write, only one book on any given topic that should be out in the world. These writers' inner critics are looking for reasons to kill their creative spark, and comparison is an easy path. Don't fall for this one, because it's just not true. Readers enjoy all kinds of writing, all kinds of stories. Another writer's success doesn't have any bearing on your success, no matter what your critic would have you believe.

Writers who fear what's on the other side of publishing: I do not want to negate any real fears here. There are writers who are genuinely afraid of people's reactions, who are sickened by the idea of their work being out in the world, even if it's the thing they want most. If you are dreading publication because of other people's reactions, find things you can do for yourself that bolster your sense of purpose, that remind you why you're doing this in the first place. The inner critic will have a field day sending you into a panic cycle of anticipation over what might happen. Try not to fall for this, and practice self-protection, like setting boundaries with people you're worried about, letting them know how you'd like to receive their feedback. You could ask, for instance, that any family member who reads your work write a letter with their feedback and mail it to you; then you can decide when or if you want to read it.

Writers whose own work triggers them emotionally: This is a tough one, because it will happen for memoirists and for any other writers who have a lot of emotional investment in their work. I include this as an inner-critic behavior, however, because I've seen too many women writers talk about their work or solicit feedback or share their writing from a place of needing to be seen and recognized, rather than from a place of owning the impact their work might have on others. Here's a simple self-assessment opportunity: Are you writing your book because you want your experience to be validated or acknowledged, or are you writing it because you want to help or support others by sharing what you've been through? If you reluctantly answer yes to the former question, that's okay, but work on letting your motivations be twofold. Work on getting away from needing that validation to come from the outside, and on cultivating it from within. If you're driven by the ways in which your book will touch others, you're already honing your self-validation skills.

Outer Critics

We cannot minimize the power of outer critics' messages when we're talking about inner critics, in part because a lot of us still have in our lives the very people (e.g., parents, family members, teachers, coaches) who lodged these original kernels of self-doubt and self-limiting beliefs in the first place. Also, because humans are complicated creatures, many of us find partners who reinforce negative messages. In addition to the people we grow up with, members of writing groups, peers, fellow students, and even children will sometimes make us feel as if we're crazy or wrong or obsessed. Actual people in our life will state out loud the very things our inner critic tells us, creating a cycle wherein we will absolutely start to see our inner critic as rational and right and sane.

Be careful! Protect yourself from your outer critics where you can. If you know you have unsupportive people in your life, don't tell them about your writing. You can say that you write or that you're working on a project, but tell them you don't want to share the details or that you'll let them know when you're finished. If you have one of these critics living under your own roof, consider writing off-site. Go to a coffee shop or a library.

Not only do outer critics reinforce the inner critic, but if you're already feeling insecure or unsure, people in your life telling you that your story is full of problems, lies, or misremembrances can cause you to come to a full stop. Worse than this is the threat that. someone will sue you or disown you. I have worked with authors (all memoirists) whose parents and siblings have threatened to sue them, whose children have threatened to disown them (and in a few cases actually have), and whose family members have insisted things didn't happen the way the author remembers them, who've denied their truths. These situations can bring a writer to her knees, and in many cases these kinds of outer critics do succeed in turning a writer off of her project, when she decides it's not worth what she stands to lose.

Novelists are protected by the veil of fiction, but that doesn't stop the critics. Some of the most intense criticism that my clients have shared over the years has come from friends and colleagues in writing programs or writing groups. For whatever reason, fiction can be more competitive than other genres, and writing programs that cultivate elitism can breed the worst kind of writer—those who do not support and champion fellow writers. Whether these writers are jealous or operating from a place of scarcity, they become outer critics, lashing out and judging, offering poisonous critiques. I've known writers who've experienced this kind of crippling feedback from so-called friends and ended up taking breaks—sometimes for years—from their writing as a result.

Where self-help or prescriptive writers are concerned, outer critics can come in the form of people who don't believe in you. I've worked with writers who are trying to stretch into their own expertise, often wanting to write a book to gain more legitimacy in their field. Just like the novelists, they're met with people in their lives who feel threatened, who question their capacity—or even desire—to write a book. It's important to identify scarcity thinking, to push aside those people—whether they're friends or colleagues or mentors or competitors—who think that there's not enough space for another book about whatever topic you're writing about. There *is* enough space. If you're being called to write and have this experience of outer critics making you feel bad about your pursuits, it's important to understand that they're out of line. It's not only unfair, but also inappropriate and usually self-serving, to squash someone's creative pursuits.

Your final experience of outer critics will come from strangers after you publish your work and release it into the world. Some writers are lucky enough not to have these experiences, but most do. Someone may criticize your writing or your story, or you may get a bad review. For women, as we discussed in chapter 2, too often these criticisms become personal, as women are criticized for who they are, rather than for what they write. I have seen Amazon reviews that have called women ugly, liars, bad mothers, man haters, and all sorts of other labels meant to take aim at their characters. The writers who are most susceptible to this kind of feedback are memoirists and writers of heavy-hitting or issue-driven nonfiction, but I've seen some of my own authors tackled by reviewers for daring to take on race, the opioid crisis, and politics.

One of my former Seal Press author is Kerry Cohen, who's written books about her former promiscuous life (*Loose Girl*), and about her son's autism (*Seeing Ezra*). Her newest memoir, *Lush*, is about her own overdrinking. When a reader sent her critical feedback, Kerry promptly posted on Facebook:

November 2, 12:58 p.m.
Becky with the opinions sent me an email.

I finished your book Lush a few weeks ago and was glad to get it back to the library. I Have never disliked a main character in any book I've read as much as i disliked you. I believe you are an entitled, affluent .,, privliedged. (Bahamas . . . really?? We'd all love to do that!!) absent mom in this book! I do believe you write honestly so i think this is who you are. How could you drink and carouse like that and be a present mother? Are you really a counselor? How in the world can you counsel people?? You seem totally screwed up to me. You have done a diservice to AA by "researching" your drinking problem. Sorry you have been such a loose girl and a lush but i dont believe you should be making money off of it . . . and in my neighborhood.
—Becky W. Hillsboro, Oregon

One form of therapy is to publicly declare, *I'm not taking this on*, in either your words or your actions. Airing the negative comments can help you set them free. Others may attempt to shame you for what you write, but your supportive community's voice is louder than all that, and they're the best medicine for the naysayers.

Daily Doses of Confidence

Over the years, I've witnessed authors with debilitating inner critics and seemingly insurmountable self-limiting beliefs go on to finish and publish their books. One of these writers stands out to me. We started collaborating in 2011, when she was working on a book about beauty and body image. Her concepts were solid, but she beat herself up every time we talked about the fact that she was not an "authoritative" voice on the topic. She could rattle off ten other writers she admired who were smarter than she was, who were better published, who had more name recognition. I reminded her that all those authors also had to start somewhere—unpublished, unauthoritative, unknown. As we worked together over a series of months, her submissions got better and better, but her massive self-doubt was crippling, and eventually she said she needed to take a break from the writing.

Two years later, she contacted me to let me know she had a publishing deal with one of the Big Five publishers. I was pleased but also stunned, given where we'd left things. "What shifted?" I wrote back in an email. "My confidence," she replied.

How she was able to turn her mindset around isn't relevant here, because I'm not about to detail a formula for going from feeling unconfident about your work to feeling confident. Every writer is different, and every book is different. This author lacked confidence because she didn't think she was as good as all the other women in her field who were better published and who had already "arrived" at the place where she wanted to be. For other writers, the lack of confidence may stem from fear of repercussions or fallout, as is the case for many memoirists. For others, there may be some old conditioning in the way—messages from family, for instance, that you can't make a living as an artist, that being a

writer is a "soft skills" job that no one takes
that it's a waste of time.

This is where the doses of confidence come in. Find
a way to prop yourself up in small ways as often as you
can. Although social media can be a toxic place, for
writers it is also a place for community building. Follow
writers you admire, join writing groups, and spend a
little bit of time each day in the company of writers.
One way this will boost your confidence is by giving you
access to like-minded people to turn to when you feel
like you're not a real writer, when you're buckling under
the weight of the critical messages. Even sometimes just
posting that you're struggling can bring a bunch of writerly types to the rescue. Try it and see.

Beyond looking outward and connecting to other
writers, also look inward. Can you say out loud, "I am a
writer"? In 2018, the She Writes team had T-shirts made
for our author retreat that said I Am a Writer. What's
Your Superpower? Ten years earlier, I would have
been mortified to wear that shirt in public. I would have
felt like an impostor, and would have been too afraid to
bring attention to myself. God forbid someone should
have asked me what I write about. Today, it's my favorite
shirt and I wear it all the time. And I love it when I go
out and people ask me about my writing, because I'm
more confident today about my own status as a writer
than I was back then. It took some time to build up to
this, as it does for anyone. These small acts, however,
get us closer and closer to believing that we are who we
say we want to be.

Push yourself out of your comfort zone, bit by bit.
Let people know you're writing. Attend writing events

and classes. Buy yourself a shirt or a piece of jewelry that signifies your commitment to your writing, or that, like my shirt, announces to the world that you're a writer. Feeling embarrassed is a form of shame, and shame keeps us from feeling confident. It makes us cower and stay small, and it makes us apologize. These are ways of being in the world that will not serve you well as you prepare yourself to become the amazing, fierce, confident writer that you are on track to become, or that you already are.

Check your default mode. If you feel embarrassed, take a deep breath. If you feel overwhelmed by feeling less-than or unworthy or unauthoritative, go for a long walk to clear your mind. If you feel shame or humiliation or fear, ask yourself where it's coming from. Give yourself a little pep talk that starts with the words *This is not mine. This is not mine. This is not mine.* You cannot erase your conditioning, but you can lessen it and you can control it, and, just like my ex-client who got the book deal with the Big Five publisher, you can find a new way of being with your writing, which means a new way of being in the world.

Here are a few exercises you might try as you explore your growing relationship with your writerly confidence:

Befriend your inner critic

This exercise involves first establishing whether your inner critic is an it, a he, or a she. Then see if you can establish some identifying characteristics of your inner critic and give it/her/him a name. Enter into a dialogue with your inner critic, asking it what it wants. You may want to do this exercise with a coach or writing buddy, with the other person asking the questions while you try to embody your inner critic. Work at this until you understand the critic's motivation. Understanding how your critic wants to protect you, help you, save you from embarrassment or failure often has the effect of making it feel a little softer around the edges.

Count your sorrys

For one day, listen to how you interact in the world. Do you say "I'm sorry" for no reason? Do you apologize by way of using qualifying statements like "But I'm not really a writer" or "I write, but I'm not a published author," or "I'm not really [fill in the blank]"? Do you apologize for taking up too much space or too much time, or even for having an opinion? Take note and be mindful. It's important to practice not saying you're sorry for nothing, and then to work on actually not feeling sorry for simply being.

Get or make an inner-critic doll

I bought an inner-critic doll on Etsy, and I love it. It has crossed-out eyes, a zipper mouth, and a bright red cape. Author Betsy Graziani Fasbinder has gotten through the writing and publication of three books with her own self-made critic doll. Betsy has written all of her critic's mean messages in Sharpie across the doll's body—on its torso, arms, and legs. This is a way to make tangible your inner critic, which allows you to separate yourself from its silly and often harmful messages. Every time I feel my inner critic wanting to say something unhelpful, I grab my doll, zip its mouth shut, and put it directly in my line of vision beyond my computer. It's fun, and it works.

Shower yourself with affirmations

One of my dear childhood friends has affirmations all over her house—on the bathroom mirrors, tucked into the corners of appliances, pegged to her refrigerator with magnets—and taped to the windows of her car. They're simple notes to self that say things like, "You shine!" "I love who you are!" "Your smile is radiant!" Every time I'm at her house, I feel better about myself because of these little notes that are so true to her that they're part of her decor. You don't have to tell yourself that your smile is radiant, but you can create some simple affirmations about your writing to support your new practice of giving yourself small doses of confidence. A few affirmations I love for writers include "You are a writer!" "Your ideas blow me away!" "Your words are powerful and will change lives!" See what you come up with. Start with a little note, just a Post-it. Slap it on the fridge and see what happens when you look at it every day. If you like it, you might decide to spread the practice throughout your house and your car.

Write as You Are

Any form of conditioning, but especially emotionally conditioning, has the power to stop writers in their tracks. Critical messages—internal and external—can and do crush new writers. In a 2019 *New York Times* book review, author Alexandra Fuller took it upon herself to eviscerate three female memoirists, the most well-known of whom was Pam Houston, for her memoir, *Deep Creek*. I came to the defense of these writers on Facebook, calling the attack what it was: gendered, vitriolic, and seemingly personal.

Houston herself wrote on the thread, "The worst thing about this review . . . is that she took out two debut memoirists, young women just getting started." This was a generous response on Houston's part, and a reminder that one does not arrive at her level without weathering the claws of critics. In this case, it was a verified literary critic, but ultimately it doesn't matter what kind of critics you face—be they your own internal demons, collective voices from your past telling you not to waste your time or not to air your secrets or not to think you're all that, or your current-day naysayers who want to tear you down or stop you or keep you in your place.

When you're feeling vulnerable, it's hard to imagine the motivations others might have to silence you, to bash the genre you're writing in, or even simply to pooh-pooh your creative efforts. It's easy to get sucked into believing these naysayers are validating what you've always known to be true—which is why it's essential to stay in your own truth and to surround yourself with positive people and supportive communities while you're in the throes of your creative process. Remind yourself that all critical messages are other people's stuff. Not even your own inner critic's message is yours to hold. You picked it up along the way, and you can choose to lay it down on the path.

To write as you are means simply to write in the now, unencumbered by what might happen as a result of your efforts—free from the baggage of past messages or future fears of what others might say or think. Writing as you are is an opportunity to write from a place of inner courage, strength, and intention. You may not always write with clarity. You may not love every word you put on the page. But you can write with self-compassion, with generosity toward yourself and your endeavor, and with conviction that you came to the blank page on purpose, and with purpose. And there, in that space of divine creation, where it's just you and your words, you alone get to call the shots.

Part II

CHAPTER 5:

Daredevil You

The first half of this book focuses on the ways in which our conditioning—and real-world circumstances—impact women's voices and women's writing and how women's writing is received in the world. Women have succeeded despite the hurdles, made strides, and pushed forward in powerful ways, but they have also stumbled and continue to be held back and to hold themselves back.

Gender identity aside, writing is challenging. What follows are some of the things I know to be true, based on my interactions with writers and authors and on my own experience:

- Writing is a creative pursuit, and there's no one right way to do it.
- Writing is a nonlinear experience, and everyone's process differs.
- Writing will bring out your inner critics, no matter how accomplished or solid you feel about your competence or your craft.
- Writing is a journey that teaches you about yourself and the world around you and helps you to make sense of your experience.
- Writing is a courageous act.

The very act of writing, if you're doing it truthfully and authentically, is an exercise in revealing yourself, exposing your underbelly, laying bare what matters to you—and because of this, it asks you to be both vulnerable and brave. There are, of course, those who wield words as weapons, who use words as shields, but they're not my focus. Here I want to acknowledge the vast majority of writers I know and work with, who write to self-express and who write books because they know, deep down, that they have a gift they want to impart to the world.

Writing and giving voice to that writing are both essential and fraught. Even for those writers who are free on the page, who write as if writing is the air they breathe, when it comes to sharing, publishing, and owning their work, the shackles can suddenly appear. Seemingly out nowhere, fear, angst, shame, and self-doubt manifest. And so our relationship with and to our writing can never be easily quantified as good or bad, easy or hard. We are *in relationship* with our writing. It can call us, tempt us, make us cower, intimidate us, force us to compare ourselves with others, make us fall in love with it and make us hate it, rile us up, beat us down, inspire us to no end, and make us feel apathetic. Every emotion you've ever experienced with another human being exists between you and your writing, because on the page you confront yourself and you confront everyone who's ever championed you or berated you, filled you up or made you feel small. In your intimate space, just you and your words, lifetimes of dynamics play out on the page, and all the things you understand and don't understand, that you know and that you're figuring out, that you suspect to be true and that you deny, begin to take shape. Then, in becoming written expression, those things are real. Things that were only thoughts become tangible, family stories get unpacked and might reveal disturbing truths, and things you didn't remember might resurface to cause grief or pain. Through your writing, you have a responsibility to yourself, yes, but you also have one to your readers. I've long held that it's valuable to have a reader in mind as you write. Ideally, it's someone who's nodding along with all the smart things you write, that supportive person in a crowd, or a new friend who finds you absolutely fascinating. It's helpful to envision this person as you write, to give yourself a confidence boost and to help yourself along when the going gets tough. Later, after you've completed a draft, you can (and should) seek out some brutally honest critics—readers or coaches or editors who will ask hard questions, poke holes in your arguments, support you to be your best. But early on, when you're tending to the embryo of an idea, when your nascent writing is forming on the page, when you're deciding to actualize your truth into writing for the first time, all you need is a cheerleader.

Over time, as you get more confident in your writing, your process will start to reveal itself. You will discover that there's a particular way in which you best get words onto the page. You'll learn that certain times of day are more productive. You'll find that you have writing quirks and habits, some of which might drive you mad, and if that turns out to be the case for you, by all means, don't let the things that drive you crazy about yourself define you or your process. For instance, you may realize that you have to create the absolute shittiest of shitty first drafts to make sense of what you have before you can really begin, or that you cannot write a chapter without first executing an outline. In short, you'll discover how you work best, which in turn will provide a container—no matter how shoddy or leaking or broken it may seem—for you to cultivate your voice.

I shared in the introduction of this book that Dani Shapiro has said that voice is courage. She mentioned this to a group of students in a She Writes University class I moderated. I asked, "What do you tell students who are trying to find their voice?" because new writers get so consumed by the idea that they must find or discover their voice. If you've taken any writing classes, you've probably heard this along the way, as if you don't already have one, as if your own voice is something you have to treasure-hunt for or that will come to you if you just try or work hard enough. Dani's perfect definition was the gem I was looking for, because in its simplicity it acknowledges two things: 1) that your voice is already in you, and 2) that the practice, or the secret, is in having the courage to let it be free.

If you're already writing, you are a daredevil extraordinaire. Don't worry if every word you write makes you feel as if you're walking a tightrope. Let any angst you might feel fuel you. If you know what it's like to hit your stride and to experience those moments when you fall in love with your words, don't take it for granted. Savor it. Remember it. That way, you have something to hold on to when those inevitable moments hit, when you post or publish something that you worry might not be well received, or when your inner critic emerges fast and furious in an attempt to take you down. You'll need to cultivate a reservoir of strength if you're pushing all the way through to whatever finish line is in your sights.

Always remember that there's enough room at the table for all of us and that each and every one of us belongs there. Writing and publishing is not a zero-sum game. There is no such thing as too much or too many of a certain story or genre. Our words are indeed gifts that we choose to share with the world, and when you make the leap to become a writer, it's imperative that you follow through, or that if you stop, you stop because you decide you're finished, or because you want to, not because of fear of outcome, or because of other people's agenda, or because someone tells you you're not qualified enough or that there's no room for your story. If you make it far enough to put pen to page, to believe you can be a writer, then you already are.

Write Like a Motherfucker

This phrase is now so popular, it's become a hashtag: #writelikeamotherfucker. For me and for many others who embrace it, tackling writing in this mindset is motivating.

It was Cheryl Strayed, author of the memoir *Wild*, whose words were the inspiration for this hashtag when she wrote the following response in her August 19, 2010, "Dear Sugar" column on the Rumpus, which she was penning anonymously at the time:

> *How many women wrote beautiful novels*
> *and stories and poems and essays and plays*
> *and scripts and songs in spite of all the crap*

they endured. How many of them didn't col-
lapse in a heap of "I could have been better
than this" and instead went right ahead and
became better than anyone would have pre-
dicted or allowed them to be. The unifying
theme is resilience and faith. The unifying
theme is being a warrior and a motherfucker.
It is not fragility. It's strength. It's nerve.[1]

I think accessing this kind of grit is important for women. After all, we know that what society expects of and values in us, including "niceness," suggests that we aren't supposed to be motherfuckers. Motherfuckers are jerks. They're more often than not men. Which is why I so love that Cheryl Strayed said this, and why the phrase has resonated with so many women. When it comes to writing, we have to write like motherfuckers to get it done. We have to be fierce and put everything we have into our work and out into the world, or we will not make it. Part of this fierceness is about surviving rejection, and about having the absolute audacity to believe we can do it—that our writing is our thing, our destiny, our right.

There are countless stories of women writers who faced whatever negativity was being foisted upon them and wrote and published anyway. In part, I'm talking about rejection, but it's a more nuanced form of rejection—because women's writing is often rejected for reasons that have nothing to do with the writing. This has been the case since publishing houses have existed, and it's truer now than ever. Yes, rejection is part of the game. It's gonna happen, period, and it will make you stronger and more discerning and more determined if you let it. But it's also essential that you not let rejection be your measuring stick, and that you not let a single person or house that might reject you determine the future of your writing career.

Madeleine L'Engle's *A Wrinkle in Time* was rejected in the 1950s by at least twenty-six publishers for being "too different," according to L'Engle herself. But she didn't change her story, and eventually she found a publisher who delighted in the novel's quirkiness.

Harper Lee's editorial team warned her that *To Kill a Mockingbird* wouldn't sell well, so Lee didn't brace herself for success. In this interview with the *Los Angeles Times*, she speaks to how extreme success can be just as scary as failure sometimes:

> *I never expected any sort of success with* Mockingbird. . . . *I was hoping for a quick and merciful death at the hands of the reviewers, but, at the same time, I sort of hoped someone would like it enough to give me encouragement. Public encouragement. I hoped for a little, as I said, but I got rather a whole lot, and in some ways this was just about as frightening as the quick, merciful death I'd expected.*

The fact is, there's a lot that's hard about writing and self-expression. It will test you, and it will make you a better person. I don't like it when writers say, "You shouldn't become a writer if . . ." You'll hear this a lot if you're a woman writer—don't write if you can't handle rejection, if you can't deal with the critics, if you don't have thick skin. I'd like to encourage anyone reading this book never to utter these words to another writer. If a writer expresses her doubts, the best response is "That's normal. Everyone feels that way." And then encourage your sisters to write like motherfuckers. Remind them that they've got this. We need to be buoyed in our moments of self-doubt, rather than having people around us affirm that we're probably right to be so freaked out and should therefore lay down what we're doing and return to real life.

A final point about writing like a motherfucker is that some people bristle at the f-word. It seems crude or crass, and if you feel this way, here's what I'll offer to you. Try saying in the mirror, "I'm a motherfucker." Seriously. Try it. My mom led a women's retreat where one of the participants shared that her daughter had gifted her a pair of socks that said, "I'm a delicate fucking flower." The woman was offended and took the statement personally, as if her daughter had gifted her these socks because she thought ill of her own mother. The woman worked through her feelings in the retreat and had a change of heart as she was able to process what she didn't like about those words, and by the end the woman was laughing and saying, "I *am* a delicate fucking flower." She got the irony and the strength and the truth of it all wrapped into one, and in embracing the message, she felt powerful.

Not everyone will want to embrace the f-word or any offshoot of it, and you don't have to. You can write however you want—like a badass, like a bat out of hell, like whatever simile you might think of that feels empowering. In my work with women writers, the biggest breakthroughs I've seen have come when a writer connects with her power. Too often, and certainly historically, women have been disempowered. Whether or not #writelikeamotherfucker resonates with you, ask yourself what boldness needs to be brought forth for you. Our voices are our power. What we say and how we say it matter. The intentions behind our sentiments have the power to affect how we write, the messages we put out into the world, and even how prolific we end up being.

Here, I simply offer an invitation to all you women writers to claim your boldness. Find what phrase or sentiment or energy moves you—and light the world on fire.

Saying No to the Status Quo

In Sylvia Plath's unabridged journals, you'll find these words:

> *What if our work isn't good enough? We get rejections. Isn't this the world's telling us we shouldn't bother to be writers? How can we know if we work hard and develop ourselves we will be more than mediocre? Isn't this the world's revenge on us for sticking our neck out? We can never know until we've worked, written."*

These musings show the insidious nature of how the world gets into our heads.

Yes, it was true, the world was telling Sylvia that she shouldn't bother to be a writer, and the world will tell you too, if you let it. Avoiding these disquieting questions means taking the easier path, but it also results in caving to the status quo.

We're saying no to all that, obviously. Even if it takes a lifetime to cultivate these nos, we're still saying no. No to those who tell us what we're doing doesn't matter. No to the idea that our writing is a hobby or a waste of time. No to our shame, even if that doesn't mean it goes away. No to those who suggest we're not going to make it if we don't toughen up, because maybe our strength lies in our vulnerability, and maybe staying open to the difficulties we must inevitably face actually makes us better writers. You can say "no, thank you" if it makes you feel better, but, women, we've got to practice our nos.

Women also need to get more skilled at refusing to carry other people's burdens, to work at not caring so much about what other people think, to take feedback at face value, and to realize that too often other people's (sometimes unconscious) agendas are in the mix. The first step toward getting more skilled is simply noticing what comes up for you when people ask you if you're still working on your book, or what happens when you're pushing and pushing and feeling like you're not getting any results. What happens when you don't receive positive reinforcement, and when you feel like you're braving this massive endeavor all alone?

Later, you'll face other ways in which the world doesn't support you. People will fail you in not giving you endorsements or reviews that they've halfheartedly promised, or in not coming to your launch events that they've RSVPed affirmatively to. I see the women authors I publish on She Writes Press going into tailspins over these kinds of letdowns. They imagine that people's not following through for them means their writing isn't good enough, that people's not coming to support them means they're not good friends. When they don't hear what they want to hear from others, or when people let them down, they weave a tapestry of stories, which may or may not be true, with themselves at the center.

While I could not find any hard evidence that suggests that women create these stories more often or in more elaborate detail than men do, I have seen in my interactions with male and female authors that women are more likely to assume a defeated position when things don't go their way. Anyone can and will feel defeated at times, of course, but watch out for it, because it automatically puts you in a one-down position, in which you assume the worst and give your power over to an idea of negativity, to lack of support, to scarcity.

A defeated position reinforces the status quo for women because women succeed when we exist in a state of abundance—with ourselves and with one another. The best way to resist a status quo that insists we are second best, or a system (and industry) that marginalizes us, is to refuse to accept that anyone else's behavior or actions has any bearing on our creative endeavors or our capacity as authors or the work we are doing in the world. Once we allow other people's reactions to inform what we do, it's not long before their reactions start to dictate what we do. And I know it's tough to be the stronger person. To weather the disappointment. To find the resources in yourself when you feel a lack of support. But do. Find a better community. Hire someone to help you through if you have to. Refuse to buy into the idea that you are not enough. When a woman writer decides she's not enough, she stops trying. She gives up on her project. She decides it's not worth it. That's a collective loss for all women, and it's a reinforcement of a status quo we're saying no to. So lead with your actions and repudiate the status quo. You can do so every day in small ways. Choose to see rejections as having nothing to do with you, to see people's lack of follow-through as fallout from their busy lives, to be more forgiving when people you wish could support you simply can't. These are not your burdens to carry, and laying them down gives you more space to cultivate creative abundance and to focus on all the open doors and the countless other ways in which people and the universe are saying yes to you.

Glorious Failure

It's a known thing in the publishing industry that men and women submit their work differently. And it's not just that men who submit as men, with male names, are more likely to have their work looked at, although this is true; men also take at face value soft rejections and any suggestion that they resubmit, while women largely do not.

In a 2015 blog post on Medium called "Submit Like a Man: How Women Writers Can Become More Successful," Kelli Russell Agodon speculated that women worry that they'll seem too pushy if they resubmit too soon. There's that "too" again—and I agree with this assessment, especially since it validates the notion that cultural (and other forms) of conditioning are part of what keep women writers back. Russell Agodon writes, "This is where many of our 'have good manners and think about other's feelings' good-girl childhoods do not serve us well." Exactly.

Rejection, even soft rejection, can feel like a form of failure, even though it's not. You're not even initiated as a writer until you face rejection.

Elizabeth Gilbert wrote in the *Huffington Post* in 2014:

> *The funny thing is that rejection is not so bad, really. This is something I think men have always understood—that a glorious failure can sometimes be more life-affirming than a cautious win. This is why men are constantly asking for stuff they might not even deserve or aren't totally qualified to handle. I don't say this as an insult to men, either; I wish more women would do the same. Because sometimes you get a yes, and even if you weren't prepared for that yes, you rise to the occasion. You aren't ready, and then you are. It's irrational, but it's magical.*

Yes, magical. But first you have to set up the conditions for that magic to be able to happen. Those conditions entail trying again and trying again and trying again. There are so many stories of authors who received countless rejections and went on to accomplish amazing things. Twelve publishers rejected J. K. Rowling's *Harry Potter and the Philosopher's Stone* before Bloomsbury picked it up for the ridiculously small advance of £2,500.

It's interesting, especially in the context of this book, that Rowling was encouraged to adopt a gender-neutral pen name to appeal to boys. She's spoken about the fact that she had mixed feelings about doing so, but at the time, she told Christiane Amanpour in an interview, "If they told me to call myself Rupert, I probably would have done it, to be honest with you." For those who don't know her story, she was a single mom on welfare before the *Harry Potter* series was picked up. By all accounts, she had failed—in her marriage, in her life, in her pursuit of what she wanted for herself and her daughter—but she stayed the course and didn't give up and is today one of the best-selling authors in the world.

Speaking of glorious failure, Margaret Atwood has shared that she might never have written *The Handmaid's Tale* if she hadn't first conceived of a failed novel. In a *Guardian* article entitled "Falling Short," she shares the story of the futile efforts she put into this novel as "making way" for *The Handmaid's Tale* to emerge. A writer could have handled this kind of experience in a number of different ways. She might have insisted that her original novel was going to work—and beaten it into submission, or have not given up on it when it was calling to be given up on. She might also have decided that in the wake of the failed novel, she didn't have it in her to tackle a new story line. She might have been too discouraged, or too tired. But, she writes in "Falling Short," "Get back on the horse that threw you, as they used to say. They also used to say: you learn as much from failure as you learn from success." True words from a very wise woman.

Confucius wrote, "Our greatest glory is not in never failing, but in rising every time we fall." Vince

Lombardi said, "It's not whether you get knocked down, it's whether you get up." And Linda McMahon said, "I have learned it's not how you fall but how you get up that truly matters."

As I wrote earlier, you don't need to heed warnings from the jaded that failure is imminent or inevitable. It is. The work is in getting back up on the horse, rising from the fall, and the way you handle the fall.

In 2018, I fell down, hard, and I have a renewed appreciation for this metaphor as a result. I was running in the hills near my home following a break-in at my office. A computer and some other electronics were stolen. I was feeling sorry for myself. One too many negative things had happened to me in a short period of time, and I decided to go for a run to clear my mind. Except I fell. And, as I said, I fell hard. My normal way of reacting to this kind of thing would have been just to brush it off, to insist that I was fine and that it didn't really hurt, and to be on my way. Another way I might have dealt with the fall that day, in the wake of so much other hard stuff going on, could have been to collapse into victim mode, wondering what I was attracting, or supposing that the universe had it out for me. Yes, it would have been really easy to go there.

I didn't do either. I didn't brush it off, nor did I bemoan my bad luck. I was with a friend, and I just let him give me a long hug. I let myself be comforted, and then I shared photos of my giant bruise with my closest friends in the weeks to come—all the way until it was healed. I marveled at how enormous the bruise was, at the power the body has to heal, and, in my own way, I turned this experience into my own glorious failure.

What's an example of a glorious failure you've experienced? And next time you fail, look at *how* you get up. Because we live in a world that forces us to get up. You will because you have to. But what happens next? How does "what happened" inform your story? How do you need it to inform your story? And how might you intentionally do things differently than you've done them in the past? How might you reframe an upsetting failure as a glorious one? The cool part is, you get to decide.

CHAPTER 6:

Women-Only

I've been lucky to spend a fair amount of time in girl-only and women-only spaces. As a kid, I did a variation on Girl Scouts called Pioneer Girls, which involved spending one evening every week with a group of girls with whom I also went to a weeklong sleepaway camp each summer. I remember mostly being happy not to have my brother and his friends around, but also, especially as we got older, I noticed how girls who at home would have been more self-conscious and more focused on their clothes and makeup stopped caring at camp. We ran wild and dirty. No boys meant freedom to play, to speak, to exist in a different dynamic where certain girls didn't try to contort themselves and others felt freer to speak up—even if only for a week.

As an adult, I attended my first women-only retreat, a leadership conference, as a college student. The opportunity was extended to me through my work as a resident assistant my senior year. I remember the strong, fierce women who were there, and also the palpable difference in the space without any men. The only voices speaking were women's voices, and it was the first time since I'd been twelve years old that I'd had that experience. The thing about women-only spaces is that they engender a different dynamic in which many women feel freer and safer to speak up and to share.

Now that I'm a working professional and I run a women-only publishing imprint and we host women-only retreats, I've seen firsthand plenty of times the magic that happens when women get together to support women. Women are connected by certain experiences, some uniquely female, like pregnancy and childbirth, and others not, like harassment and rape. But all women react to men's energy—and they do so in very different ways. Some women get more assertive, some more submissive. Some try to impress, while others seem to fall into unconscious gender roles or want to blend in to the wallpaper. In my experience, removing the male element seems to create a more neutral field, and often, as a result, women are willing and able to go deeper and get more personal than they otherwise would.

I'll share two personal examples to show how men's energy and orientation toward women impact space. These are often small, subtle things, but they're small, subtle things that women don't have to deal with when we're only in spaces with other women.

The first story I'll share comes from a 2017 trip to New York City for the publishing trade event Book-Expo. I was invited to have drinks with two male colleagues. We went to a local bar, ostensibly to talk about distribution. What ensued was what I would call flirtation, at best, on the part of one of the men. If I'm being gracious, I'll say he thought he was being charming, or perhaps gregarious. But he was persistent in his questions about how much I liked to party and whether

I loved alcohol, and in his assumption that I liked to get high, even though nothing about my behavior pointed to any of these things. I'd ordered a single glass of wine, and the only factor that could have prompted this last supposition was that I live in the Bay Area (home to much marijuana).

After his relentless sexual innuendos, I finally disclosed that I had been married to (and recently divorced from) a woman, hoping that this information would cause him to lay off a bit, but he just doubled down. He yelled, "Oh my God! Why didn't you tell me?" As if we were intimate. As if we were having drinks for any reason other than to talk about business. I hadn't wanted the conversation to get personal, but it had from the get-go. He'd insisted that it go that direction, goading me on about partying, drinking, smoking pot, and ultimately my sexual orientation. Needless to say, I didn't like it, and since I didn't feel bold enough to flat-out tell him how uncomfortable he was making me, I ultimately just stood up and said I had to go.

The second story is about something that happened at a She Writes women-only retreat. We invited a single man to sit on one of our panels. He was in fact the only man in the room, and his first comment, as he held the mic, was that he had never been in a room with two hundred women. Okay, so there were only about eighty of us, and it was an innocuous enough comment. Some of the women giggled—a trained response that I've definitely given in to on occasion when men have said things that I didn't know how to react to. But later, when one of the older women in the audience asked him to speak more loudly into the microphone, he responded, "Why don't you come up here and sit next to me, sweetheart?" Then he patted the seat next to him.

The four other women on the panel, including me, stiffened up but said nothing, because to call someone out for a comment like that would have made more of the situation than was called for. After all, he was just being friendly, right? So it was no big deal. But the fact is, it *was* a big deal, and several women later commented on the #MeToo moment that had played out onstage at our women-only retreat.

Men like this are often forgiven, for being clueless, for being old school. And part of me gravitates toward the question of whether it is a big deal. There's a lot of talk going on, in the aftermath of #MeToo, about the shades of gray surrounding "bad behavior." My feeling is that if it's worthy of an eye roll, it's probably not worth making a public spectacle, but the fact that it's incumbent on women to make that judgment call is frustrating and upsetting—not to mention that we have been trained to accept, or at least to endure, this kind of behavior. We just suck it up, over and over and over again.

In professional contexts, the degree to which these kinds of small, subtle interactions wear down our authority is immeasurable. It's difficult to assert authority when someone is sexualizing you. It's hard to be on a level playing field when a man is being patronizing. It's nearly impossible to navigate these situations with grace. The best way I know to deflect bad behavior is with humor, and I know only a handful of women who are big enough badasses that they just call shit what it is—consequences be damned. I've seen that these women get a lot of respect, but for a lot of women, making these calls in these kinds of situations goes against the very core of who we've been raised to be. If you're like me, you've succeeded in some instances and failed in others. So it's a work in progress, but we should all aspire to find our voice when we know something doesn't feel right.

Why Women-Only?

Women-only environments emerged during the 1970s, when women who were part of the second-wave feminist movement started to claim public space as an act of resistance against patriarchal culture. Starting in the late 1960s, consciousness-raising groups cropped up, starting in New York and quickly spreading to other states. These were generally local get-togethers where women went around the room and talked about issues they faced.

The modern-day version of this concept is a talking circle, which is not gender-specific but which follows important rules that inherently value equality. According to the guidelines for talking circles, "each one is equal and each one belongs. Participants in a Talking Circle learn to listen and respect the views of others. The intention is to open hearts to understand and connect with one another."[1]

I got to participate in a talking circle in late 2018, when I saw the play *Gloria: A Life* in New York City. After each show, based on the life of Gloria Steinem, a prominent person or activist led a talking circle. I was privileged enough to attend on a night when Gloria herself was the leader.

One of the more insightful moments in the play is when Gloria, played by actress Christine Lahti, reaches her later years and discusses her mentorship with Wilma Mankiller, the first woman elected to serve as principal chief of the Cherokee Nation, who tells Gloria how the Iroquois Indian tribe's traditions were the basis for the US Constitution. In the version of the play I saw, actress Brittany K. Allen, playing Mankiller, spoke of talking circles as "a consensus among women and men," as "a paradigm of human organization [that is a] circle, not a pyramid."

Women inherently gravitate toward these more circle-like spaces, finding themselves lost or silenced in the pyramid structure, where they automatically fall to the base. It's no surprise, given Gloria Steinem's life experiences, that she would be drawn to talking circles for the structure they set up, where rules forbid people to talk over one another, where everyone listens and respects other people's time and what they're sharing. She's spent her whole life weathering criticism for anything and everything. I've read that she was stunned by the negative criticism she received for her 1992 memoir, *Revolution from Within*. She told *Interview* magazine, by way of defending herself to the critics, "I was saying that many institutions are designed to undermine our self-authority in order to get us to obey their authority." This may have seemed radical at the time, but in today's politics, this undermining is in plain view, and we seem to be further away than ever from the circle style of leadership.

Women-only spaces sprang up as a way for women to share, but also to be heard. In a pyramid style of leadership, those relegated to the base are not heard. They are not seen. Women-only spaces grant women permission and visibility in spaces where those benefits have previously been denied, ignored, or dismissed. The controversy that exists around women-only spaces is a form of backlash (which we discussed in Chapter 2). There's increasing visibility around men's rights groups, who are using a lot of the same tactics that women used in the women's movement. The difference, of course, is that women were actually fighting oppression in the women's movement, so when men today claim that they are victims or somehow gender-disadvantaged in a culture that favors them in every possible way, it's hard to be sympathetic.

Since 2016, because of the polarization and radicalization we're experiencing in the United States, there's been markedly more visibility in the men's rights movement, whose adherents reject, among other things, any notion that men are privileged relative to women. It's hard not to draw a connecting line from this emboldened group to a smattering of recent lawsuits against women-only events in the 2010s. In 2017, they were brought in New York City and Austin against movie theaters hosting women-only showings of *Wonder Woman*, and in Los Angeles against comedian Iliza Shlesinger, who posted online, "No Boys Allowed" for one of her shows. This prompted two male provocateurs to purchase tickets and show up to see what would happen. They were at first allowed in, but after they left and tried to come back, they were refused entry. That they then became litigious begs the question of what they were trying to achieve from the get-go. In a piece on HelloGiggles.com, Karen Fratti wrote, "The frustrating thing is that [these men] attempted to get into the show, . . . as far as we can tell, *because* [they] wanted to be turned away, provoking controversy where there didn't have to be any."

Because She Writes Press publishes only women authors, I occasionally get an email from an angry man. Sometimes the subject line implies the content: "Do you publish men?" Mostly these are neutral inquiries. More often than not, the man on the other end asks me if he can change his gender or publish under a pseudonym, bemused by the joke that I've heard a hundred times. Sometimes men are quick to tell me how much they love women, as if our exclusion of them implies they don't love (or, more important, support) us. It does not. Or as if loving women disqualifies a man from being a misogynist. The two are not mutually exclusive.

In 2017, I got an inquiry from a man whose resentment was palpable. He informed me in a very officious way that he'd endorsed a She Writes Press book and therefore found it "ironic" that we don't publish men. He implied that his support of a female-authored book should cause us to rethink our very mission, which I found presumptuous.

I attended a book reading shortly after I got that angry email, at which women read from their personal essays, most of which showcased experiences of repression, abuse, and disadvantage. A brave man in the audience stood up during the Q-and-A portion and asked, earnestly, "How do you write your personal stories without being overcome by rage toward men?"

I felt at once grateful for and compassionate toward his position. In my experience, most women are not actively angry at men. We're angry at the internalized sexism and gender biases that hold us back and keeps us in second-tier situations. We're angry at a culture that so disdains women's empowerment that it undermines our efforts and advances. We're angry at specific men who spew hateful comments about women's appearance and menstrual cycles as a way to propagate gender differences, suggest that all that matters about women is how we look, and purports to write us off as overly emotional or hysterical for the fact of our biology. Curious and open male allies will find great friendships within women-only circles if they can simply accept that we not only need these communities but have earned them.

Women have sought each other out for support and championing, and we've created alliances and networks and sisterhoods because the same wide-open roads that exist for men do not exist for women. Because men actually are privileged relative to women. Because the world actually is scary for women.

A fabulous song went viral on YouTube in October 2018, following the Kavanaugh hearings and a defensive comment from Donald Trump: "It's a very scary time for young men in America right now." Lynzy Lab's song, "A Scary Time," is full of ironic lyrics about how hard it is for young men in America but ends on this serious note: "It's not such a scary time for boys / They've always had the upper hand / They've always had a choice."

So, yes, women-only spaces matter and are needed—in schools, in publishing, in mentorship programs, in industries everywhere. Women, claim them. Men, accept and champion them. Sometimes I think about all the men who challenge me for having a women-only publishing platform and consider what it would be like if equal numbers of men—hell, any men—would write and say thank you for creating a women-only publishing platform to give women a voice. What if one of the men who endorsed one of our books simply shared, "I loved that book. I was so happy to be able to lend my name to it"? To me, She Writes Press's biggest contribution lies in its elevating women's voices. Equality is not a zero-sum game. Women's getting ahead doesn't compromise men's power. All we do when we elevate women's voices is normalize the reality that women do get ahead, and that we're as capable as men of doing so.

Dismissed

In *How to Suppress Women's Writing*, Johanna Russ wrote, "If women's experience is defined as inferior to, less important than, or 'narrower' than men's experience, women's writing is automatically denigrated. If women's experience is simply not seen, the effect will be the same."

That women's books are considered "narrower" than or inferior to men's books is one insidious way in which we end up valuing books by women less than those written by men. Feeling dismissed is a frustrating experience in any capacity, but where writing is concerned, it's particularly infuriating because it's so commonplace, a collective and unconscious bias that has real-world consequences for women writers.

In a *New York Times* piece called "The Second Shelf: On the Rules of Literary Fiction for Men and Women," novelist Meg Wolitzer told a story of meeting someone at a party and getting around, as we do, to talking about work. The man she was chatting with asked her if he'd have heard of her work, to which she responded with her name and he didn't recognize it (no biggie, she acknowledged), but then he pressed her about what her books were about. When she replied, "Sometimes they're about marriage. Families.

Sex. Desire. Parents and children," he called over his wife, because she was the one who read "that kind of book." Wolitzer observed, "When I look back on that encounter, I see a lost opportunity. When someone asks, 'Would I have heard of you?' many female novelists would be tempted to answer, 'In a more just world.'"[2]

In the title essay of *Men Explain Things to Me*, Rebecca Solnit told a somewhat similar story, but with a more aggressive partygoer, whom she described as "an imposing man who'd made a lot of money." In their conversation, it surfaced that she was a writer, and he asked what she wrote about. She chose to focus on her most recent publication, a book about Eadweard Muybridge, an English photographer known for his pioneering work in photographic studies of motion. As soon as she mentioned the name Muybridge, the partygoer cut her off, holding court about a "very important Muybridge book" that was just out, which he had not read but had read about.

Even as Solnit's friend stood by, trying to convey to this man that he was talking to the author of *that* book, he continued on, not hearing or recognizing that Solnit was an expert on the subject, the author of the very book he was pontificating about, until finally, the third or fourth time the friend told him it was Solnit's book, the man understood and his face went ashen.[3] This would be an amusing story if it weren't so painful.

Dani Shapiro shared a story in *Still Writing* that explained the title of the book. An artist friend pulled her aside at a dinner party and told her that someone asked him if he was still doing his "sculpture thing," to which he pondered to Dani, "How was I supposed to respond? 'Are you still doing that brain surgery thing?'"

Shapiro wrote of being asked by both strangers and acquaintances whether she was "still writing." She mused, "It always felt, to me, like a shameful thing that I was being asked this—that surely if I had written more books, won more awards, made more money, was better known, I wouldn't be dealing with this question. *Still writing?*

As it turned out, Shapiro wasn't alone. She asked around and discovered that all kinds of artists encounter this question—even award winners and household names. She concluded with what she would like to say, maybe what she would say next time someone asked: "Yes, yes, I am. I will write until the day I die, or until I am robbed of my capacity to reason. Even if my fingers were to clench and wither, even if I were to grow deaf or blind, even if I were unable to move a muscle in my body save for the blink of one eye, I would still write."[4]

Women writers who find themselves in similar exchanges may want to use some variation of Shapiro's defiance the next time someone says this to you. You might feel compelled to justify your writing as worthy or valuable. You may be made to feel as if your work is not valuable—just a little hobby or sideshow. You may even achieve success and still demur, not owning that success, or qualifying it as not a big deal, or even going so far as to be self-deprecating or self-denigrating. How we think about our own work—whether in reaction to others' comments; or how we feel about our work as a result of other people's observations, opinions, and judgments; or our own internalized critical voices—actually propagates this problem of how we get dismissed.

Olivia Sudjic's 2018 book-length essay, *Exposure*, is an examination of the kinds of behaviors women experience when others invalidate their work. She experienced crippling anxiety and blamed herself. But as the essay persists, she unpacks the ways in which women writers are invalidated on the grounds of sex. She writes about how women writers are scrutinized for writing things that are rigorous and dismissed when they write subjects that "belong to them," noting, "It's maddening how it's both presumptuous for a woman to write beyond her limits (invariably those of her own experience) and equally presumptuous to write about or from that experience."[5]

For some writers, being dismissed or invalidated inevitably leads to feelings of shame. When Christine Blasey Ford testified to the Senate Judiciary Committee in 2018, all I could think about were the countless memoirists I've worked with over the years who still blame themselves for the things that happened to them. Although the statistics state that one in every four women in sexually assaulted, the majority of women have experienced some form of sexual harassment or sexual assault that falls short of rape. Women's memoirs often tell of harassment, sexual impropriety, sexual assault, and sexual abuse as a result. I have yet to work with a memoirist disclosing these kinds of truths who doesn't grapple with whether she'll be believed, or whether she has the right to tell her story in the first place. Unfortunately for us, what Ford's brave testimony showed us is that we do indeed have something to fear. We can put ourselves out there and tell the truth of what happened to us and then be excoriated for our efforts.

When I interviewed Mary Karr for a Berkeley Arts & Letters event in 2016 as part of her tour for *The Art of Memoir*, I asked her a question about how it felt once her books were out in the world and published. I had assumed she would say it was a relief, that she'd spoken her truth and that the act of publishing her memoirs was somehow a means of letting go of the burdens she carried. Not so, she explained: "Mostly, it was a lot of discomfort. I always feel ashamed when I turn [the manuscript] in. I just feel ashamed. I think, *This book is horrible*. It's worthless. And then by the time I have to go on the road, I've sort of accepted what the book is. It's as good as I can make it, and I've just let it go."

That shame is so deeply a part of the female story speaks to the prevalence of abuse in our culture, which is why the #MeToo movement has been such a colossal and important cultural phenomenon. *New Statesmen America* reported that in the first week of #MeToo, "1.7 million tweets included the phrase, and 45 percent of Facebook users in the US had at least one friend who posted 'me too.'" A 2018 Stop Street Harassment survey on harassment and assault concluded that 81 percent of women and 43 percent of men have experienced some form of sexual harassment or assault in their lives.

Women writers I was working with when #MeToo started felt relieved that these stories were surfacing in ways they hadn't before, and they felt an urgency to tell their stories and a refreshing validation of the experiences that they'd kept buried, often for decades, fearing the fallout, fearing they wouldn't be believed. There was a certain shock of recognition of just how prevalent harassment and abuse have been in people's lives. Where previously they'd dismissed, ignored, or buried these stories, suddenly writers were beginning to wonder not only *whether* these stories mattered, but *how* they mattered—how these stories shaped them, riding under the radar to sabotage their confidence, their sense of self, their voice.

Now that the initial outpouring has abated, we have enough distance to consider some of the broader implications of the #MeToo movement. One is that people are abusing power in every arena of life, and in every industry. And I say *people* because it's the case that some of these people are women. #MeToo is about people who abuse power, but a MarketWatch story attempting to quantify the number of male versus female perpetrators offered some interesting and nuanced reporting about the fact that men are less likely to report incidents of sexual assault or harassment, about the disparity of abuse by men and women, about the fact that sexual abuse is about power over and therefore about who has the power—mainly men, but not only men.[6]

For those writers who are writing true stories about their #MeToo experiences, other complications are in the mix. I've heard women suggest that no one wants to hear another #MeToo story. I've heard industry people say that there's no more room for #MeToo stories—that we've saturated this space. But to me this is another form of dismissing. To suggest to women that they're too late because other stories and books have been published on the subject, or that they cannot or should not bear witness because that's "been done," is one of the more disturbing cultural messages I can think of. As writers, we should never be limited or censored by what's already been done, just as we should not be limited or censored by the person who perpetrated the abuse (or their colluders, which include those who may have allowed or ignored the abuse, or those invested in protecting the abuser's legacy or memory). As Anne Lamott famously said, "If people wanted *you* to write warmly about them, *they should have behaved better.*"

Do not buy into the message that your voice doesn't matter. Just because others have spoken doesn't mean your story has been told. Just because there are other abuse memoirs on the market doesn't mean you should put your desire or need to write your own book on hold. Just because there may be fallout in the aftermath of speaking your truth doesn't mean that you have to be responsible for other people's feelings.

Whether or not you publish your truth, at least write it. Tell it to someone. You don't owe anyone your silence. In fact it's quite the opposite—you owe yourself the freedom to say what happened, out loud, unfettered, unburdened.

Women-Only Writing Spaces
AROHO
http://aroomofherownfoundation.org/
An online hub encouraging creativity and relieving isolation

BinderCon
https://bindercon.com/
A convention in NYC and LA

Black Women Playwrights' Group
http://blackwomenplaywrights.org/home.asp
This community gathers in multiple cities.

The Coven
https://www.thecovenmpls.com/
A community space in Minneapolis

evolveHer
https://www.evolveher.community/en/
A creative workspace in Chicago

Hedgebrook
https://hedgebrook.org/
A global community surrounding a residency in Washington state.

Hera Hub
https://herahub.com/
Spa-inspired coworking spaces in multiple cities.

HerStories Writers
https://www.herstoriesproject.com/start-here/
A writing and publishing community tailored to Gen-X women at midlife

The Hivery
https://www.thehivery.com/
A creative coworking space in Mill Valley, California.

Kitchen Table Literary Arts
http://www.kitchen-table.org/creative-writing-society.html
An online community supporting women writers of color

Portland Women Writers
https://www.meetup.com/Portland-Women-Writers/
A meetup group in Portland, Oregon.

Quilt
https://www.wearequilt.com/
This community gathers in different meeting places in multiple cities.

Redbud Writers Guild
https://redbudwritersguild.com/redbud-writers/
An online community of Christian women creators.

Scottsdale Society of Women Writers
https://www.meetup.com/
Scottsdale-Society-of-Women-Writers/
A meetup group in Scottsdale, Arizona.

She Writes
SheWrites.com
An online community for women writers.

Society of the Lark
Women's Writing Circle
http://wvwriters.org/home/
writers-groups-around-the-state/
Subgroups of West Virginia Writers

Tall Poppies
https://tallpoppies.org/for-readers/
A group of authors and a way to connect with readers.

Tender

http://www.tenderjournal.co.uk/

A quarterly journal made by women

The Wing

https://www.the-wing.com/

Women-only workspaces that are not strictly writing spaces.

Women's Fiction Writers

http://womensfictionwriters.com/about/

Blog and editing/coaching services.

Women's Fiction Writers Association

https://www.womensfictionwriters.org/about-wfwa

Community of writers of women's fiction.

Women Who Write

https://www.womenwhowrite.org/about

Community of women writers who meet in various locations in New Jersey.

WomenWriters

https://www.womenwriters.net/

A place to publish online for free with a built-in community of readers.

Women Writers, Women's Books

http://booksbywomen.org/
about-women-writers-women-books/

An online literary magazine.

Women Writing Berlin Lab
https://www.wearewwbl.com/about/
A writing community for women in Berlin.

Women Writing for (a) Change
https://www.womenwriting.org/
Writing circles, classes, and retreats in
Cincinnati, OH.

Women Writing the West
http://www.womenwritingthewest.org/
A community of writers sharing stories of the
Women's West.

Writing Life
http://www.maryannmoore.ca/circlesevents/
A six-week women's writing circle.

Women-Only Book Publishers

Affinity Rainbow Publications
https://affinityrainbowpublications.com/index.
php?main_page=about_us
An ebook and POD press focusing on lesbian
literature.

Aunt Lute Books
https://www.auntlute.com/
A nonprofit multicultural women's press based in
San Francisco.

Bella Books
https://www.bellabooks.com/
Publisher of fiction for and about
women-loving-women.

Belladonna
http://www.belladonnaseries.org/
A feminist, avant-garde collective promoting women
and feminist writers.

Boudicca Press
https://boudiccapress.wordpress.com/
Publisher of brave & powerful writing from women of
weird fiction

Bywater Books
https://www.bywaterbooks.com/about-bywater-books/
Publisher of lesbian fiction

Desert Palm Press
http://www.desertpalmpress.com/index.html
Publisher of lesbian fiction

The Feminist Press
https://www.feministpress.org/
Publishes classic and new writing, aiming to elevate
silenced and marginalized voices.

Headmisstress Press
http://headmistresspress.blogspot.com/
Press aiming to promote and market lesbian-identified
poetry.

Herself Press
https://www.herselfpress.com/
Press aiming to revive the work of women writers from the North of Ireland.

Honno Press
https://www.honno.co.uk/
A press that only published work by women of Wales.

Inanna Publications
https://www.inanna.ca/
Canadian press dedicated to feminist voices.

Intaglio Publications
http://www.intagliopub.com/authors.html
Publisher of lesbian fiction.

Kelsey Street Press
http://www.kelseyst.com/
A press founded to address the marginalization of women writers

Kore Press
https://korepress.org/
A press that provides a progressive platform for diverse literary work.

Linen Press
https://www.linen-press.com/
Independent publisher in the UK for women, by women.

Modjaji Books
http://www.modjajibooks.co.za/
Independent feminist press that publishes southern
African women writers.

Mother's Milk Books
https://www.mothersmilkbooks.com/index.php
A family-run press that celebrates femininity and empathy

New Victoria Publishers
http://newvictoria.com/index.php
Lesbian feminist press.

Paris Press
http://www.parispress.org/
A press aiming to publish groundbreaking yet
overlooked literature by women writers.

Perugia Press
https://www.perugiapress.com/wp/
Publishes the winner of the Perugia Press Prize for a
book of poetry by a woman.

Resolute Publishing
http://www.respublishing.com/
Publishes books by women of color, focusing on
African American and/or LGBT works.

Sapphire Books
http://www.sapphirebooks.com/
Publisher of lesbian literary works.

Seal Press
https://www.sealpress.com/
Publisher for women writers and feminist issues.

Shade Mountain Press
http://www.shademountainpress.com/about.php
A publisher dedicated to publishing marginalized
women that challenges the status quo.

She Writes Press
http://shewritespress.com/
A hybrid press for women created as a response to the
barriers to traditional publishing

Spider Road Press
http://spiderroadpress.com/
Small press specializing in writing by and/or about
strong, female-identifying folks.

Spinifex Press
http://www.spinifexpress.com.au/About_Us/
Australian publisher that focuses on feminist and
literary works with several specialties.

Spinsters Ink
http://www.spinsters-ink.com/
A press committed to giving voice to women writers
from every walk of life.

Switchback Books
http://www.switchbackbooks.com/

A press producing and promoting books of poetry by women.

Three O'Clock Press
http://www.threeoclockpress.com/about-us/
A Canadian press devoted to ground-breaking feminist writing.

Triplicity Publishing
http://www.tri-pub.com/submissions
Publisher of Lesbian Fiction.

Virago
https://www.virago.co.uk/
An international publisher of books by women.

Wicked Publishing
http://www.wickedpublishing.net/
A publisher focusing on lesbian literature and LGBT and mainstream fiction.

With/out Pretend
http://www.withoutpretend.com/
Canadian publisher of works by women-identifying writers and visual artists.

Womancraft Publishing
http://www.womancraftpublishing.com/
An imprint dedicated to sharing powerful messages by women, for women.

Women Unlimited
http://www.womenunlimited.net/default.htm
Non-profit feminist publisher in India and South Asia.

Ylva Publishing
https://www.ylva-publishing.com/
Publisher of books about women loving women in a variety of genres.

Zubaan Books
http://zubaanbooks.com/about-zubaan/
Publisher of books by and about women in South Asia.

Women-Only Bookstores

BookWoman
https://www.ebookwoman.com/
Feminist bookstore in Austin, Texas.

People Called Women
http://www.peoplecalledwomen.com/
Ohio's only feminist bookstore.

The Second Shelf
https://www.thebookseller.com/news/
rare-books-dealer-launches-journal-and-shop-
dedicated-female-authors-845721
Feminist bookshop in Soho featuring rare books and "future classics."

Women and Children First
https://www.womenandchildrenfirst.com/

Bookstore in Chicago promoting writing of women and other marginalized voices.

Womenscrafts
https://womencraftsptown.com/
Lesbian owned store promoting work of female artisans, authors, and musicians.

Other feminist bookstores that also sell male authors:

Antigone Books
https://www.antigonebooks.com/
Bookstore in Tucson, Arizona run and owned by women.

A Room of One's Own
https://www.roomofonesown.com/
Bookstore in Madison, Wisconsin with roots in the feminist community.

Bluestockings
http://bluestockings.com/
Volunteer-powered bookstore, fair trade cafe, and activist center in the Manhattan.

Charis Books and More
https://www.charisbooksandmore.com/
Independent feminist bookstore in Atlanta, Georgia.

CHAPTER 7:

Sisterhoods

When SheWrites.com was just a seed of an idea, cofounders Kamy Wicoff and Deborah Siegel dreamed of an online community that would mimic writing salons they'd attended, where there was always an abundance of energy and inspiration, and also support for other writers. In an article Deborah wrote on the new site when it launched in 2009, she said, "Friends don't let friends write alone." By the time I started She Writes Press with Kamy, that sentiment was practically legendary, and yet I remembered what she'd written as, "Writers don't let writers write alone." It stuck with me that way probably because the kinds of writers I want to be in community with don't necessarily have to be my friends, but we do have to have the same values: a spirit of abundance, the belief that a rising tide lifts all boats, and a heartfelt desire to support other writers (and therefore not let them write alone).

When I invited Deborah to be a guest on the *Write-Minded* podcast I cohost with Grant Faulkner of NaNoWriMo, I asked her about community—what she notices about writers she works with who embrace community, versus those who don't, and what the difference is for those writers. She observed that the willingness to tap into community, which means to contribute and not just to ask, creates a more effective writer. If you approach communities with a "have-to" energy, the engagement, beyond not being sincere, won't help you. She laid it on the line: "Be effective in community, or don't bother."

I endorse this way of thinking wholeheartedly, although this isn't a condemnation of those people who don't want to engage with communities. It's not for everyone, and some people don't have the bandwidth. But when you decide you're ready, be prepared to engage. If you're already oriented toward participation and involvement in community, then you know that the biggest reward comes from having a broader holding for your experience. Within community you'll find support, commiseration, people to celebrate your successes and hold your hand and your heart through your failures. Within community are other people who've walked similar paths and will let you know you're not alone, give you much needed pep talks or pats on the back, or sit with you while you lick your wounds. This writing thing in particular is tough to weather alone, so I don't recommend doing it. I encourage you to find community, and the good news is that your people are out there. So show up, introduce yourself, and then engage by sharing yourself and offering support to others. That's the entire process of reciprocity in a nutshell.

In Mark Nepo's book about community, *More Together Than Alone*, he writes about one of the most famous communities around, Alcoholics Anonymous, and honors AA for its commitment to fellowship. He writes, "To invoke the humility that so much is beyond our control widens our compassion. To restore our belief in something larger than ourselves, regardless of what we've been taught, enlarges our acceptance of life."[1]

These precepts are true in writing, too, because the best writers show up with humility. The most honest ones will admit to getting beaten up by their writing process and will share the complexities of their relationship with their writing. The most compassionate writers will share with you their own struggles and help you to feel less alone in your journey. I am fortunate that my own community of writers, both She Writes Press and SparkPress authors, exemplifies the very best way to be in community with other writers. Our private Facebook pages are some of the most incredible testaments to humility, grace, support, and compassion I have ever seen. When a writer posts her fears, the amount of honest sharing that's forthcoming is beautiful to behold. When a writer posts her gratitude, gratitude comes back to her tenfold. When a writer shares a win, the support she receives is genuine. When a writer posts an event or asks for a sister to join her for a panel or a festival, she will find someone to meet her out in the real world, where the ripple effect of the online community results in even deeper, in-person connections.

I am grateful beyond measure for the community values that were already in place at SheWrites.com before I came onto the scene. And what I've learned about community in my seven years with She Writes Press is how truly little it takes to be involved and how truly supportive communities are always there. They welcome you back even if you take a break. I've learned over these years how eager people are to share their hard-earned wisdom, and that if someone can spare you from making a misstep they've made, they will. I've seen how writers can and do live in a state of abundance, rather than scarcity, where another author's win is their win, rather than a perceived slight or loss. The very best communities are those that make you want to be the best version of yourself because the members lead by example, and that kind of support and encouragement is contagious.

Sharing, Collaboration, and Why Not to Write Alone

I know that I create better in collaboration. I think this is true for a lot of people, maybe most people, because we do not create solely for ourselves. There are reasons and seasons to write for ourselves alone—to record what we're going through, to sort things out, to make sense of our experiences—but ultimately writing is a communal act, because of the very normal human *impulse to share*, which stems, I think, from a desire to be seen. In *More Together Than Alone*, Nepo writes, "The impulse to share what we gather is at the heart of all community. For sharing what we know and what we hold sacred knits the torn fabric of the tribe."

Writing is a solitary act. Even if you write in community, you alone are putting pen to page, fingers to keyboard, and no one else can transmit their thoughts onto your page, nor would you want them to. But once you become a writer, once you set out to share your words—whether on social media or a blog post or in the form of a book in progress—the act of writing takes on a bigger purpose. Then your writing is something that will be seen, and that you want to be seen, even if it brings up feelings of abject terror or shame. Lots of writers write things they don't intend to publish, things that scare them to death for fear of exposure. Yet, I've seen how these scariest of episodes are sometimes the ones that writers most long to share, too—things like abuse, rape, neglect, bad parenting choices, abortions, and addictions that result in suffering and loss. These are things that carry shame, or that have been buried and unseen, and in releasing these experiences, writers feel free.

One of my favorite books from my time at Seal Press is Amy Ferris and Hollye Dexter's *Dancing at the Shame Prom: Sharing the Stories That Kept Us Small*, whose very premise is that writing and sharing your shame will set it free. I caution you to examine yourself and make sure you're ready to set your experience free, but once you are, there's nothing more powerful than the absolute power of healing that comes from knowing that whatever you were holding on to is not your secret to hold anymore.

Leo Tolstoy wrote, "Art is the passing of feelings from one human heart to another." This is what writing is all about. And those feelings don't have to be pretty or calm or wise. They can be messy and chaotic and unresolved. The reason we're beckoned to the blank page in the first place is that we believe we have something to impart. We want to share it. We write it down. Only then do we begin to fret about who will see it, how it will get out into the world, whether it's good enough, and all the rest. Before all that angsting consumes you, let yourself sit with the sentiment that Tolstoy identified and see whether it rings true. Do you hope to pass something from your heart to another's? I imagine the answer for anyone writing as a form of self-expression is yes. Perhaps not for the author of a technical manual, or an academic text, but perhaps so. Even authors whose goal is to disseminate technical information may want their readers to be moved, even if only intellectually. But for writers of fiction, of personal story and memoir, of poetry, of creative nonfiction, we are hoping to move readers' hearts and souls as well—one human heart to another. Holding this intention is a beautiful way forward through the fear.

Another guest on the *Write-Minded* podcast in 2019 was Laura Lentz, a writer and teacher on Kauai, Hawaii, who teaches a process she calls "syncreation"—the act of writers creating together, in sync with one another's energy. She shared on the podcast how this works, how when she gets writers writing together, the amount of synchronicities (also part of the "sync") that happen is astounding and magical. She shared about a time when the Golden Gate Bridge showed up in four of her students' pieces, and another time when a red bicycle played a role in three students' work.

Every writer has her own process, a way in which she practices her craft. If writing in collaboration is not currently part of your process, give it a try. This doesn't mean you have to write in a roomful of people to practice syncreation. There are many ways in which you can write with others, or with others in mind. In November 2018, when I was in the throes of finishing this book and doing NaNoWriMo to try to push through a lot of content, one of my best friends died. She'd been living with amyotrophic lateral sclerosis (ALS) for six years, so it wasn't a surprise, but I was still floored. It derailed my November writing for a full week. But when I picked back up again, it was with Sarah by my side. She was in my heart and my mind and my writing space. Because this book and its subject matter are for the Sarahs of the world—courageous women writers who sometimes need extra encouragement, who need an occasional reminder of how awesome they are, since the outside world isn't always going to pull through for them—I leaned on my Sarah as a collaborating partner. She was in my space as I finished this book, and in many ways championed me all the way to the finish line.

Some of you have experienced your biggest champions not being alive. They may be a parent, an aunt or uncle, a sibling, a teacher or mentor, or a friend who's passed, who would have been your biggest cheerleader and who you wish were around to see your accomplishments and celebrate your success. But those folks are still here for us, and we have access to them. All you have to do is invite them to be a witness.

Writing with others or with others in mind is collaborative. And collaboration will help you think better. Having a witness makes your arguments stronger and your writing clearer. Holding someone in your heart and your mind also holds you to a higher standard. Find good partners to support you along the way. If you know you're passing your feelings from one heart to another, be mindful about who you collaborate with. Find the right partners for your different stages of the journey, but trust your impulse to share and to impart your gift to the world.

Competition and Envy

I once worked with an author who actually stopped talking to her friend Cheryl Strayed because she was jealous of Cheryl's success. Of course, she didn't frame the story this way when she told me about their falling-out, but I could see through it, given the timing and circumstances of Cheryl's rise to success. In the years since, I've felt sorry for this author, because who wouldn't want a powerhouse like Cheryl in her corner?

Women need to cultivate and tend to our relationships with other women, to prop up our sisters when they succeed, because their success is our success. Another writer's success does not mean less potential success for another writer, because a readership is not a finite resource. During the 2018 midterm elections, some Democrats were up in arms about Beto O'Rourke's fundraising feat, even going so far as to suggest that he should give some of the $38 million his campaign had raised to other Democratic candidates in closer races. Plenty of pundits called bullshit on this way of thinking, arguing that the people who gave money to O'Rourke were moved to contribute by O'Rourke and O'Rourke alone. They weren't even necessarily dyed-in-the-wool Democrats who would have donated to the candidates in those other, closely held seats. O'Rourke had inspired them, period. The *Washington Post* reported this wrongheaded comment, which seemed to epitomize the thinking of a lot of political operatives at the time: "Every dollar that's going to Beto is a dollar that is not going to Florida or Montana or North Dakota."

The reason I share this anecdote is that this is the definition of scarcity thinking, and it reminds me of the kind of thinking I see happening in book publishing.

Beto O'Rourke is like a best-selling author. People are buying what he has to say because they like him, they like his words, and they like how he articulates himself. People have more money to spend, but they want to spend it on messages they want to hear, messages that resonate. The same is true in publishing. If you have something someone wants to read, it doesn't matter who else is out there doing what you're doing. Someone else's success does not mean you start in a hole. So I feel for this ex-friend of Cheryl Strayed's, because she did it all wrong. Instead of championing Cheryl and being a steady hand for her, she resented her and lost someone who could have been a source of support.

If you allow yourself to believe that other books out there similar to yours, or someone else's success, is contributing to your inability to rise, you are stuck in a psychology of lacking that promises to hold you back from your goals. One of the biggest assets we have as writers are our connections. The writing world is ultimately very small, and connections matter. My advice to all writers, but especially women, is to hold on to your friends. Cultivate writerly relationships. Be generous. And if you get sucked into an envy spiral, do everything you can to give yourself a pep talk out of it. To experience envy is to be human, so don't feel bad when you experience it, but try to understand it for what it is. According to *Psychology Today* columnist Mary C. Lamia, envy is an emotion "directed at another or others, wanting their qualities, success, or possession[s]," and it stems from shame. Knowing this can allow for some helpful self-inquiry. If we can allow ourselves to go there, we can address the manifestations of shame—addiction to approval, hypersensitivity to rejection, feelings of not being good enough, taking things personally, all-or-nothing thinking—for what they are and then move on.

The hosts of the podcast *Call Your Girlfriend*, Aminatou Sow and Ann Friedman, have a brilliant concept they call Shine Theory, which is loosely based on lyrics from the Killers song "Read My Mind." Friedman wrote in *The Cut*, "Surrounding yourself with the best people doesn't make you look worse by comparison. It makes you better." Writers can practice Shine Theory every day by propping up other writers. We talk about karma. We say, "What goes around comes around." We encourage people to pay it forward. These things are part of the cultural conversation not because they're trite expressions or actions, but because they're true.

Befriend magnificent women writers. Let yourself be inspired. Champion others' success, even if it means that you experience a little bit of envy from time to time. In contrast with the story of the author who unfriended Cheryl Strayed, Elizabeth Gilbert shares in her book *Big Magic* a sweet story of having friended Ann Patchett. She saw Patchett give what she calls a "robust and dazzling" speech, and when Gilbert introduced herself to her afterward, she said to her, "Ann, I realize we've only just met, but I have to tell you—you're extraordinary and I love you!"

This is how you do it. Let yourself fall in love. Allow yourself to be open to the possibilities of friendship and support and amazing, wild connection that can be there when you believe there's a spot for you at the table alongside women you admire. There's not a finite number of seats. And the only person who can make you feel as if you don't belong there is you.

A New Way of Thinking About Mentorship

The idea of having the right mentor can sometimes bring stars to aspiring writers' eyes, because they equate that relationship with future introductions to agents and editors, or they imagine that their mentor will impart to them the secrets of the writing and publishing universe.

In the real world, it's true that having a mentor can be life-changing or life-affirming. Many writers espouse the benefits of their mentorships—people they credit with having opened doors, taught them the ropes, introduced them to key players along their publishing journey. Sometimes these relationships are canonized, and I think that gets authors nostalgic, if people can be nostalgic for a time and experience they never went through (though if anyone can do this, it's writers). Henry James was a great champion of Edith Wharton's just as she was starting her writing career and he was ending his. Their work showed up in some of the same literary journals, and she sent him a copy of her first book of tales, *The Greater Inclination*, in 1899. While he was initially unimpressed, he reached out to her in 1900, after reading her short story "The Line of Least Resistance," writing, I brave your interdiction & thank you both for your letter & for the brilliant little tale in [*Lippincott's*] . . . I applaud, I mean I value, I egg you on in, your study of the American life that surrounds you.[2]

More recently, Jonathan Safran Foer has credited Joyce Carol Oates as a mentor, telling *New York* magazine in an interview, "She made me believe that I had talent, which no one had suggested to me before."

These two examples showcase relationships more than one hundred years removed from each other. Given the chapter on history that kicks off this book, it seems important to note that men have always advocated for women, and that women can mentor men, too. Also notable is that, try as we might, we can't always choose our mentors. For instance, Wharton may have sent James her book in hopes that he'd have a reaction, but initially he was not inclined to support her. Still, she did the right thing by putting herself on his radar. And oftentimes our mentors choose us, as was the case with Oates and Safran Foer.

I've found that for all the talk that goes on about the value of mentors, few people know how to actually pursue them, and many of the women I work with try to forge these would-be connections in abrupt and awkward ways. If you know you want to work with someone, start by working with them. Attend classes or workshops they teach. Go to an event where they're speaking or reading, and introduce yourself and let them know what you admire about their work. Don't foist your vision of their becoming your mentor upon them until you actually have a relationship with them, and don't expect them to see you as special at that first meeting.

Because of my own network of high-profile writers, authors ask me all the time to make connections on their behalf, but these kinds of introductions always feel like they come with an agenda: The writer in question wants something from the high-profile person—a blurb, at the very least, or sometimes more. And particularly if mentorship is in mind, then I would say an online introduction is simply not enough, especially for authors who are in demand.

While mentorship should eventually turn into a friendship, a supportive system wherein the mentor champions the mentee, don't think for a moment that a mentorship can't start as a paid relationship, or that it can't start small. I mentor a lot of writers, and almost always they start out as my students and clients. In 2017, a woman reached out to me after seeing me speak at a conference and let me know that she'd determined that I was going to be her mentor. I read her impassioned email, and was even moved by it, but she was asking me for writing coaching, which is something I do for a fee. I didn't have a connection to her, other than having met her at the conference, so I felt clear in my response that she should enter into a coaching relationship with me. When I explained that this would happen at my normal rate, she balked. But I wasn't looking for a pro-bono client, and if I had been, I wouldn't have chosen her. My point here is to be careful about your expectations and what you put on people, and to be mindful, when what you're asking for might seem unreasonable to the person you're seeking to mentor you.

Where starting small is concerned, you can plant the seed of a potential mentorship relationship by following someone on social media, commenting on their posts, and sharing their stuff. Part of getting yourself on the radar of a potential mentor is to practice acts of generosity. You don't have to fawn all over the person you admire, but you can and should sincerely champion them first if you have an expectation that they'll champion you.

I've seen a few articles in the wake of the #MeToo movement suggesting that men feel reluctant to mentor women. I hope this is a fleeting, knee-jerk reaction that will pass, because this kind of hesitation will do a huge disservice to men and women everywhere in the long term. That said, some of the abuses of power that have come to light have occurred between mentors and their mentees, unfortunately, so it may take time to sort through the wreckage. Book publishing has had its share of disturbing revelations of famous men taking advantage of their positions of power. In reading those stories, you see women entering into relationships thinking they're getting access, which turns out not to be the kind of access they want.

Sherman Alexie, likely the most famous Native American writer alive, was accused of (and has admitted to) trading on his literary celebrity to lure women into uncomfortable sexual situations. Sociologist and self-proclaimed feminist Michael Kimmel, the only cis-male author Seal Press ever published (*The Guys' Guide to Feminism*), experienced massive fallout after a number of his former graduate students accused him of being sexually inappropriate and sexist, and of making transphobic and homophobic comments.

In children's book publishing, a 2018 Medium post by Anne Ursu blew the lid off an entire segment of the industry. She wrote:

> *In December, I opened a survey about sexual harassment in children's publishing. . . . I received almost 90 responses, as well as emails and DMs from people who didn't want to fill out the survey because they felt too ashamed, or were still frightened of reprisal.*

These stories break my heart because the writers in question wanted to be taken seriously for their work and believed they'd found allies. On NPR, Ursu poignantly noted, "If you are an aspiring author, and you go to a reading of someone who is famous and beloved and whose work you admire, and he suddenly takes an interest in you and your work, and he thinks you're special, and you start emailing, and he wants to mentor you—and then suddenly it turns out all he wanted to do is have sex with you, those writers are left utterly devastated.

When mentors break the bonds of trust with their mentees and abuse their position to elicit sexual favors, or to insist that women pay to play, so to speak, the devastating result is silencing, or worse. The women carry a secret they didn't ask to be burdened with, and the pain these experiences cause has, in some cases, turned women away from their craft altogether. When we look at these abuses and their ripple effects, the losses become too great to quantify.

I think writers would do themselves a favor to think about mentorship in a less targeted way. Instead of seeking particular mentors or feeling as if you should be making connections to people who can open the next door for you, consider the type of people you'd like to have in your inner circle and why. You might cultivate as mentors authors you love just because you read their work, not because you know them. If you're learning from someone and you admire them, it doesn't really matter if they know you or specifically support you. You can still call that person a mentor.

Having mentors and being successful in your pursuit of mentorship has a lot to do with setting expectations. Courtney Martin, author of *The New Better Off*, has a wise and generous post on *On Being* in which she shares the art of being mentored: 1) Express your gratitude early and often; 2) make your mentor's life easier in some small way; 3) your mentor is not your mother; 4) don't expect perfection from your mentors; 5) create a team of mentors; and 6) be brave (which is about being true to yourself and listening to your own instincts).

I would add to these six points not to aim for the stars when it comes to who your mentor should be. Sometimes our mentors are our peers. Sometimes we can be in a relationship in which we are both mentor and mentee. And sometimes our mentors have less life experience than we have but offer us specific and unexpected gifts.

In 2019, the world of book publishing is highly competitive, and we're told that to make it, we have to be connected and know people and have a bajillion followers and fans. The pressure is enormous, and I think a lot of authors are looking for a quick hit by striking some sort of mentor jackpot. Instead of looking for that magic bullet, I would offer to any new or aspiring author that what you're looking for is in the communities out there that are ready and waiting for you to join them. Start attending conferences. Meet the presenters, but also meet the participants. Go to classes and connect with teachers and students alike. Participate in online forums and Facebook groups and writing communities. Leave comments. Get to know people. Retweet people's stuff. Like their comments online. Practice daily acts of generosity, and within a short period of time, you'll discover that you have unwittingly created a whole team of mentors. I see mentoring in the new publishing landscape as being about how you engage with people and who's in your inner circle, even if that circle is virtual. The authenticity and courage you bring to any community, online or offline, manifest themselves in the form of organic connections that are less forced and as rewarding as, or even more rewarding than, any fantasy about the perfect mentor of your dreams.

CHAPTER 8:

Amplify

Once you have wrestled with your courage and set your voice free, the necessary next step toward claiming your spot at the table involves amplifying your voice. Luckily for us, our multimedia culture gives us plenty of opportunities to do so, but for a lot of writers the pressure to amplify and put themselves out in the world triggers anxieties and the kinds of messages that are connected to the conditioning we addressed in the first half of this book. It's one thing to write, but it's quite another thing to push your words out in front of people, not only because it's exposing, but also because it activates other responses in us: the desire for our work to be well received, the hope that people will respond, the anticipation that some powerful gatekeeper will anoint us and our work and from there we'll follow the publishing journey of our dreams.

I know well the complex emotions that surround writers' putting their work out into the world. The act is full of paradoxes, because shame coexists with a deep desire to be seen, fear of not being good enough lives alongside the wish for the work to become a best seller, and impostor syndrome lurks there in the corner, even as you begin to feel as if your words have the power to change lives. I'm less interested in why writers live in this state of paradox and much more interested in the fact that the only way through the shame, fear, and insecurity is to do the work—over and over and over again. I know writers who have been writing and publishing for years who still feel shame and fear and insecurity bubble up every time their work goes out into the world. But they push through it, and they do it anyway—and this is what we're all required to do if we want to amplify.

From time to time, women I meet tell me that they write just for themselves, that they have no personal ambition to publish, that they get full satisfaction from the act of writing alone. It's not that I don't believe this story, but my guess is that their ambition is in fact buried, and that somewhere along the way, they bought into the idea that writing for themselves was enough. Encapsulated in this belief is a little story that stars a woman who doesn't try to outshine anyone and who resists being too big for her britches. She knows where her priorities lie. It's fine if she pursues the "writing thing" as a hobby, and if she were to publish, it would just be a legacy project for her kids. Sounds okay, right? But I would like to crumple this little story and throw it in the trash can, and if you've stuck with me all the way through to the final chapter of this book, then I hope you'll want to join me in setting the pages on fire, because this story keeps women small. It attempts to tamp down the creative energy pulsing inside us. It works to prevent women from dreaming too big. So, if this is your story, let's see if we can shift the narrative to its having been your story, and move right along.

Amplifying your words is your ticket to the next, better thing you're going to be doing with your writing, and even with your life. There are countless pathways to getting your words into the world—on social media; via podcast, radio, and video; and of course through the publication of digital and print books. There are also countless strategies for authors who want to amplify their voice. It's important to determine for yourself up front how important it might be for you to pursue the traditional publishing path, because if that's your goal, you must have, or commit to building, a substantial author platform (which we'll discuss more in this chapter), and even then, it's tough—really tough—to get an offer from a publishing house. If you decide to opt out of traditional publishing and pursue independent publishing, then you have a menu of choices that include DIY self-publishing (doing a lot or most of the work yourself), assisted self-publishing (hiring a consultant or team to assist you in self-publishing), hybrid publishing (an author-subsidized option for writers who want some of the benefits of traditional publishing, like marketing and distribution), and hiring a service provider (a company you pay for self-publishing services).

Gone are the days when an aspiring writer wrote a manuscript, tried to get an agent or a publisher, waited for whatever gatekeeper to say yes or no, and then either got their work out in the world or put the manuscript into a drawer. Today's publishing landscape is so different from what it was twenty years ago that it's unrecognizable to authors who come back after a hiatus. The measures are different than they used to be, mostly in that what's appealing to publishers about potential authors has more to do with the authors themselves than with the content of their books.

You—the author—drive your author platform. The things that comprise the author platform are all the ways in which you put yourself out into the world. They include but are not limited to your social media, your mailing list, video and audio content, teaching and speaking, connections to high-profile people, and previous publications. If you're looking at this list and thinking, *I've got none of that*, then you're a good candidate for independent publishing. Get a book out into the world and use that book to build an author platform, and then buckle down, because the business of becoming and being an author really is a full-time gig.

Regardless of how you publish, your success hinges on your energy for what you do, and on the commitment you make to your book's success. In *Almost Everything*, Anne Lamott writes, "No one cares if you continue to write, so you'd better care, because otherwise you are doomed." This sentiment continues to be true once your book is published, because no one cares if you continue to promote, either. While these are harsh words—or tough love, depending on how you receive them—it's also helpful to be armed with what to expect. The journey of launching your work into the world is a lot like running back-to-back-to-back marathons. You have to have stamina to keep going; you need to be steady and consistent, or you will burn out; and you must take the necessary breaks when you need them, always keeping in mind that once the break is over, you're going to get back out there and continue what you've started.

Three Publishing Success Stories

My last book, *Green-Light Your Book*, was all about how and why to say yes to yourself as a writer, and about the various paths to publishing that exist for authors today, and about encouraging people to publish and publish well. I'm not going into that level of detail in this book, but my feelings about publishing are as clear-eyed as they were when that book came out in 2016, and my feelings about the state of book publishing are as sober as they were in 2012, when I left traditional publishing to start a nontraditional press.

For readers who don't know my position on publishing, here it is in a nutshell: Traditional book publishing is more risk averse than ever. If you hope to get a deal with one of the Big Five publishers—Penguin Random House, Simon & Schuster, HarperCollins, Macmillan, or Hachette—you must have a strong author platform (or be famous or know famous people). If you don't have one, you must build one, and getting to the level that makes you attractive to a big house will probably take you five years.

Beyond the big houses are the small houses, and if you're the kind of author who has a niche project, you may be perfectly suited for a small house that might take a risk on you, even if you have a small platform, because your content is a perfect fit or because you seem like the kind of author that imprint wants to cultivate. If this description fits you, identify the houses you want to publish on and send editors there heartfelt query letters explaining why their house is a good fit for your book and what you bring to the table. Do not bother with agents if you're approaching small houses. Agents are going to want to go for the Big Five and will support you with small houses only if they've exhausted the big houses first, and if they still believe in your project enough after that to keep submitting. You must articulate to small houses what you bring to the table. If you don't have anything, you need to work with a coach or consultant to figure that out, or consider publishing independently.

When I talk about publishing independently, which I also call alternative publishing, because it's not traditional, I'm referring to the myriad publishing paths I mentioned at the outset of this chapter: DIY self-publishing, assisted self-publishing, hybrid publishing, or hiring a service provider. This is where the majority of debut and returning authors (the ones I mentioned who were easily published in the 1980s and now find that the publishing world has spun off its axis) will find themselves, and it's a good place to be. Most first-time authors, especially if they don't have a platform, will not get a traditional book publishing deal. Understanding that this is the case up front is helpful in dispelling the myth that there's anything wrong with your work if agents and editors aren't interested, or if they tell you they don't think they can sell enough copies to justify taking it on. The simple truth is that publishing is contracting. There are fewer and fewer publishers and more and more authors. Publishers cannot take risks on unknown authors, and the yardstick they're using to measure your potential success is a lot heavier and more stringent than the one you might use to measure your own success.

There's a lot of creative control for authors who take the independent route, and a thriving indie author community waiting for you if you choose this path, so don't think for a second that choosing to be an independently published author makes you second best. In my opinion, it makes you entrepreneurial, and, most important, it means you're saying yes to yourself, getting over whatever potential barriers are keeping you from taking the next step toward authorship and all the wonderful rewards that come from being a published author.

I want to share three stories of women who pursued different publishing journeys, all with a tremendous amount of work and discipline, and all to great effect. I'm inspired by Glory Edim, whose online moniker is Well-Read Black Girl. I had the privilege of sitting on a panel at BinderCon with her in 2016, and I was struck by her singular focus of elevating black women writers. Edim's anthology, *Well-Read Black Girl: Finding Our Stories, Discovering Ourselves*, was acquired by Ballantine and came out in October 2018. But this didn't happen because Edim had a good concept and got the book deal—far from it. She had a vision to create a book club and digital platform that celebrated the uniqueness of black literature and sisterhood. In fall 2017, she organized the first-ever Well-Read Black Girl Festival, and compiling an anthology fell into place from there. Edim did the hard work of building her author platform to justify her book's acquisition by a Big Five publisher.

The reason Edim inspires me is that she never lost sight of the big picture. She got the publishing deal of her dreams, but she also stayed true to what she set out to do from the beginning. In a 2018 NPR interview, she said, "The voices in the anthology are really thought-provoking and unique. We need to have an array of different stories and voices, especially as black women, because there's so much we have to offer to the world."

Ryka Aoki is an Asian American trans woman who, by her own account, was primed for a mainstream literary career. A poet who obtained her MFA from Cornell and imagined she'd follow in the footsteps of T. S. Eliot, she had a vision of what the future would look like.

Quickly, however, the realities of book publishing caught up with her and she realized that the work she wanted to put out into the world wasn't mainstream and that big presses did not want to take her on. She told me in an interview that she saw two choices ahead of her: 1) to hide in her bedroom, or 2) to be a revolutionary and a fighter.

She started making a name for herself by reading and performing her stories in public. That led to her getting a few short fiction pieces published—the beginning of her author platform. She saw that her work was for a niche audience and began not only to accept that reality, but also to embrace it. "It takes a bit of maturity," she said, "realizing that you're playing a different game." Aoki published her first book, *Seasonal Velocities,* on a friend's press where everyone involved was gender-variant, and that appealed to Aoki. Within a small community of fans and readers, she became known. Her second book, *He Mele a Hilo (A Hilo Song)*, was a novel about being an Asian woman who lives in Hawaii. She sent it to an LGBT publisher in New York City that wanted to publish it. She noted that this was a novel without explicitly LGBT content, and she appreciated that her readers were receptive to content from her that didn't specifically deal with gender issues.

Aoki speaks about her third book, *Why Dust Shall Never Settle Upon This Soul,* as an act of giving back. She told me about how she chose to support Biyuti Publishing and its founder, a trans woman of color, as a way to do her own work and bring someone else up in the process.

The result has been rewarding for Aoki. Publishing on small (niche) presses has meant letting go of the dream of being T. S. Eliot, but that's morphed into a new dream: publishing what she wants, on her terms, with supportive publishers and readers who support her work, even as she crosses genres and explores subjects that speak to her heart.

Andrea Jarrell is a She Writes Press author who opted out of traditional publishing from the get-go. In her case, her reasoning had more to do with time and effort than with anything else. She'd heard too many horror stories about traditional publishing from friends—stories of loss of creative control, long time-lines, bad relationships with agents and editors—and decided she didn't want that. She wanted to take her publishing destiny into her own hands, so she chose to publish her memoir, *I'm the One Who Got Away*, with She Writes Press. I'll also say that She Writes Press chose her, because, as a hybrid press, we have a vetting process that makes for a collaborative partnership between author and publisher. But Jarrell's success stemmed 100 percent from her approach. She believed in her book. She believed her book was good enough and that she was deserving. She chose her publishing path with pride, and her results were astounding. This slim and beautifully written memoir got media attention on par with that of any traditionally published book, if not more so.

I see Andrea's success as stemming from the combination of her powerful story, her publicity, and her attitude.

I have no doubt that the Big Five experience would have been less gratifying for her. She might have gotten a book deal, but she would have been subject to the whims of the house, perhaps chosen as one of its lead books, given more attention and publicity dollars, but perhaps not. For authors who want to exert some control over what actually happens to their books through the publishing process and afterward, independent publishing has a lot to offer.

In 2018, I read a *New York Times* article about book publishing that was so stunning in its simplicity and naïveté that it reminded me of how myopically some people still think of book publishing, and how little the average person understands about how much it's changed in the last fifteen to twenty years. The article, "How to Finally Write Your Nonfiction Book," provides very little nuance about publishing, and suggests, as I've seen in other articles about book publishing, that authors just need to decide whether they want to publish traditionally or self-publish. The author, Kristin Wong, writes in the first paragraph, completely skipping over *how* said book might get published in today's competitive environment, "Once your book is published, the work is far from over: You must now sell it like your life depends on it, because it kind of does." Later in the piece, she circles around to this "decision" authors must make about how to publish, not addressing how competitive the traditional space is and omitting all of the many "third-way" publishing options that exist for authors, like hybrid publishing, assisted self-publishing, and hiring service providers to support with publication.

I'm troubled by these kinds of articles because they do aspiring authors a disservice with their lack of information and by selling a dream about traditional publishing that is no longer. Yes, book deals still happen. Yes, if traditional publishing is what you have your heart set on, then go for it. But in my own TEDx talk, "Green-Light Revolution," I talked about how, at some point, you might need to set aside that dream, and in doing so you can make room for a new dream, one that has the same potential for success. There are many ways to do this thing right, so just because you've always imagined a scenario in which an editor at a traditional house falls in love with your work and offers you an advance, and you move from there to best seller–dom, make sure not to let that fantasy dictate how you measure your success. And especially don't let the rejections that are inevitable along the traditional publishing journey determine your publishing destiny.

Stake Your Claim, Claim Your Voice

There has never been a more interesting time in the history of book publishing. There have been other disruptive times, and times of great growth and change, but never before have individual writers had so much control and choice. Earlier in this chapter, I addressed why control and choice are such a big deal for women writers. We struggle with worthiness. Some women don't get to make financial decisions that prioritize their wants and needs. Most of us suffer from some or all of the forms of conditioning that we talked about in the first half of this book. Yet, despite the fact that all of these variables exist, we're still writing and publishing, and our sisters are setting examples for how to do it right and giving us blueprints to follow if we choose to harness this control and choice and manifest our publishing destinies on our own terms.

Few events are more life-changing and soul-affirming than offering up your work in the form of a published book. The act of creating a story, honing your words into a message that matters to readers, or honoring your truth by recording your experience in memoir form is a way of telling the world, *I am here. I have something to say. I have something to impart. I want to share with you a story, a message, a truth.* You are passing feelings from one human heart to another.

We all know what it feels like to receive this passing of feelings. We've felt it in our own favorite books, books that might have saved us when we were young, given us permission at some point in our lives, or assured us that we were okay and helped us to carry on through during difficult times. I think because we have this experience as readers, we have a desire to continue the passing-on of feelings. To originate those ideas and to be the one who's doing the passing is one of the most gratifying parts of publishing a book and having people read it. Hearing back from readers about how your words touched them is one of the most profound things an author will experience.

My goal when I set out to write this book was to help women see their own awesomeness. Even the writers I know who have healthy egos and who do truly feel worthy of publishing still sometimes wrestle with the fallout of conditioning, because it's impossible not to. You were raised in a culture that mirrored for you the ways women are supposed to act and what we're valued for. You've been subjected to slights, double standards, and being passed over. You've experienced sexual discrimination and harassment, and you're among the minority if you've escaped worse—abuse, assault, violence. Being a woman in this world is an exercise in finding the courage, over and over and over again, to exert our voices, to challenge the status quo, to find it in ourselves to say yes (because no one else is going to). We have to pat our own backs and pull ourselves up and be the champions of our own dreams. If we're very lucky, we find sisters and a sisterhood. If we're very lucky, we beat our conditioning through the support of amazing people in our lives, and because we do the things we're afraid of and we see how doors open, how people listen, how we are valued—and that affirms what was always true: Our voices do matter, and what we say has merit, and speaking up and out is the only way forward.

There are so, so many stories of women who've risen to great success because they either refused the answer the culture (or the industry) was giving them or refused to be confined or controlled by messages (internal and external) that would hold them back.

Issa Rae, author of *The Misadventures of Awkward Black Girl*, is an amazing example of someone who had all variety of cultural barriers flying her way but refused to be deterred. Before she was an author, she was trying to make it in Hollywood with her web series by the same title. But she had trouble getting attention because people in Hollywood didn't get her. She had to contend with the very real hurdle that content from a black woman's point of view was not a hot commodity. Ultimately, her series went viral, and she raised money through Kickstarter to complete and launch it on YouTube. As of 2019, her channel has more than four hundred thousand subscribers. Issa essentially bypassed the gatekeepers who didn't understand what was appealing about what she was doing, and while today she's entrenched in more traditional structures, she's earned the right to continue to do less conventional things, writing for and starring in her HBO series, *Insecure*, and by all accounts claiming her place at the table on her own terms.

She Writes Press author Sandra Joseph writes in her book, *Unmasking What Matters*, about her sometimes debilitating impostor syndrome. This renowned singer, who was *The Phantom of the Opera*'s longest-running leading lady, writes:

> *Even after landing the role of Christine, I was nowhere near impervious to the criticism of others—or my own self-doubt. Many nights in my dressing room at the Majestic, that fire escape beckoned, and it took everything in me not to succumb to its siren call. Why? I was the leading lady of a huge Broadway hit—the fulfillment of my lifelong dream. I was, by every external marker, a success. And yet, rather than celebrating this achievement, my fear of not being enough just morphed into impostor syndrome.*

For Sandra, as with so many women writers I've worked with over the years, this same niggling self-criticism and self-doubt wove their way into her writing process. Again, there she was, hitting every marker of external success but getting sucked back into that too-familiar vortex. I'm happy to say that Sandra is really good at naming what's going on—after years of practice—and in so doing was able to recognize the impostor syndrome for what it was. She did everything right when it came to her book and her book launch. Undoubtedly, she had to talk herself through some of the knee-jerk moments when that familiar voice rose up to ask its boring old question— Who do you think you are?—but Sandra's answer was clear. She's an author. She's living her purpose. She's not letting anything stop her. And she's a role model for all authors who struggle with these messages. Name what's going on, and move right along into your brilliance.

I want to return to the #MeToo movement for a moment because its very existence has spurred such an outpouring of stories and essays and books from women who didn't previously think they had a story to tell, or who didn't understand how resonant their stories of abuse or survivorship might be to others. I've been sharing a lot of stories of individual writers who've created their own success, who've overcome obstacles to publish their work and to make their writerly dreams a reality, so I don't want to lose sight of how these bigger collective movements propel us all forward, too. When we speak up and out, we raise all women. When we support and champion women writers, we advocate for the advancement of all women writers and also for ourselves.

Writing is an act of courage, and it doesn't matter how small you start. You might find yourself feeling compelled to share some part of your story in a Facebook post, or you might find a more formal outlet, like a literary journal or a blog, or maybe you'll choose to save everything you have for the book you've always known you want to write. Do whatever feels right. Follow the thread of your voice. Trust the courage that propels you forward. Envision yourself at the table. Name your authority to be there and choose the chair that best suits you. Sit down, lean back, cross your legs, and kick off your shoes, Sister. This isn't a formal boardroom setting, after all. This is your life.

Michelle Obama, on a book tour for her memoir, *Becoming*, in late 2018, said in one of her interviews, "I have been at probably every powerful table that you can think of. I have worked at nonprofits, I have been at foundations, I have worked in corporations, served on corporate boards, I have been at G-summits, I have sat in at the UN. They are not that smart."

The reason I love this moment of honesty is not that she's being a little snarky or letting us in on a big secret, but that she's reminding women that we may be setting the bar too high for ourselves. We're the ones thinking we don't get a seat at the table, when in fact we do. We may turn over the word "authority" in our minds and on our tongues and feel that it doesn't suit us. That we're not that powerful. That we don't deserve it. That we're not big enough.

Remember this: Real power comes from authenticity of expression and incremental, small actions that effect change. No one determines who's deserving in this life, so you've just gotta reach out and grab hold of the belief that you are. And big enough is a state of mind. Each day is a growth opportunity, a chance to stretch forward into uncomfortable territory, to leap into a bigger vision, to say yes to opportunity, to double down on your commitment to yourself and to what matters. You can't will away the shame, the fear, or the insecurities, but you can choose courage over them. You can take the next small step. And you can remind yourself, until it sinks in deep, that your voice is many things: a tool for change, a blade to cut through the noise, a song that inspires, a potion that casts a spell, a portal to another world, a light in the darkness, a steady hand along a hard journey. So do what you're going to do and get out there and use it.

Notes

Introduction: This Is Our Time

1. My use of the word *women* throughout this book includes trans/nonbinary and genderqueer women.

2. Briony Harris, "What Is the Gender Gap (and Why Is It Getting Wider?), *World Economic Forum*, November 1, 2017, www.weforum.org/agenda/2017/11/the-gender-gap-actually-got-worse-in-2017.

Chapter 1: She Wrote, She Writes

1. Rebecca Smith, "A Day in the Life of Jane Austen," *History Extra*, December 15, 2016, www.historyextra.com/period/georgian/a-day-in-the-life-of-jane-austen/.

2. Hilary Marland, "The Yellow Wallpaper: A 19th-Century Short Story of Nervous Exhaustion and the Perils of Women's 'Rest Cures,'" *Conversation*, February 27, 2018, https://theconversation.com/the-yellow-wallpaper-a-19th-century-short-story-of-nervous-exhaustion-and-the-perils-of-womens-rest-cures-92302.

3. Wendy Martin and Sharon Becker, "Writing as a Woman in the Twentieth Century," *Oxford Research Encyclopedias*, July 2017, http://literature.oxfordre.com/view/10.1093/acrefore/9780190201098.001.0001/acrefore-9780190201098-e-764.

4. Rachel Blau DuPlessis, *Writing Beyond the Ending: Narrative Strategies of Twentieth-Century Women Writers* (Bloomington, IN: Indiana University Press, 1985); Sydney Janet Kaplan, book review of *Writing Beyond the Ending*, in *Signs* 13, no. 3 (spring 1988).

5. Virginia Woolf, *A Room of One's Own* (London: Hogarth Press, 1929).

6. Deborah K. King, "Multiple Jeopardy, Multiple Consciousness: The Context of a Black Feminist Ideology," *Signs* 14, no. 17 (autumn 1988).

7. Langston Hughes, *The Collected Poems of Langston Hughes* (New York: Alfred. A. Knopf, 1994).

8. Zadie Smith, "This Is How It Feels to Me," *Guardian*, October 13, 2001, www.theguardian.com/books/2001/oct/13/fiction.afghanistan.

9. Rindy C. Anderson, Casey A. Klofstad, William J. Mayew, and Mohan Venkatachalam, "Vocal Fry May Undermine the Success of Young Women in the Labor Market," *PLOS*, May 2, 2014, https://journals.plos.org/plosone/article?id=10.1371/journal.pone.0097506.

10. Elise Solé, "Christine Blasey Ford is being shamed for having vocal fry—here's what that is," Yahoo Lifestyle, https://www.yahoo.com/lifestyle/dr-christine-blasey-ford-shamed-vocal-fry-heres-181504246.html.

11. Elaine Showalter, "Women Writers and the Double Standard," *Ars Femina*, https://arsfemina.de/woman-sexist-society/women-writers-and-double-standard.

Chapter 2: Writing Under the Influence of Gender
1. Kim Parker, Juliana Menasce Horowitz, and Renee Stepler, "Americans See Different Expectations for Men and Women," *Pew Research Center*, December 5, 2017, www.pewsocialtrends.org/2017/12/05/americans-see-different-expectations-for-men-and-women/.

2. Rhiannon Lucy Cosslett, "How to Refocus the Spotlight on Female Writers," *Guardian*, November 1, 2018, www.theguardian.com/books/2018/nov/01/how-to-refocus-the-spotlight-on-female-writers-joyce-maynard-olivia-sudjic.

3. Nicole Froio, "On Holding Women Memoirists to an Unfair Standard," *BookRiot*, September 6, 2016, https://bookriot.com/2016/09/06/on-holding-women-memoirists-to-an-unfair-higher-standard.

4. John Bonazzo, "Twitter Challenge Proves Male Authors Don't Know How to Write About Women,"

Observer, April 2, 2018, https://observer.com/2018/04/male-authors-write-about-women-twitter.

5. Catherine Nichols, "Homme de Plume: What I Learned Sending My Novel Out Under a Male Name," *Jezebel*, August 4, 2015, https://jezebel.com/homme-de-plume-what-i-learned-sending-my-novel-out-und-1720637627.

6. Mike Thelwall, "Book Genre and Author Gender," *Wiley Online Library*, December 21, 2016, https://onlinelibrary.wiley.com/doi/pdf/10.1002/asi.23768.

7. Aamna Mohdin, "Women Are Horribly Under-represented in the World's Top Literary Awards," *Quartz*, November 17, 2016, https://qz.com/838175/the-national-book-award-and-other-top-literary-prizes-seriously-under-represent-women/.

8. Nicola Griffith, "Books About Women Don't Win Big Awards: Some Data," *Nicola Griffith*, May 26, 2015, https://nicolagriffith.com/2015/05/26/books-about-women-tend-not-to-win-awards/.

9. Susan Faludi, response to #BacklashBookClub, *Medium*, September 12, 2014, https://medium.com/matter/the-summer-of-backlash-f2c63df0c5b0.

Chapter 3: A Woman Must Have Money
1. bell hooks, *Feminist Theory: From Margin to Center* (New York: Routledge, 2015).

2. Jane Friedman, "Writing for Love (and Money),"
Vimeo, May 3, 2014, https://vimeo.com/97144156.

3. Carrie V. Mullins, "The Disastrous Decline in Author
Incomes Isn't Just Amazon's Fault," Electric Literature, January 11, 2019, https://electricliterature.com/
the-disastrous-decline-in-author-incomes-isnt-just-
amazon-s-fault.

3. Richard Nash, "What Is the Business of Literature?,"
VQR, spring 2013, www.vqronline.org/articles/what-
business-literature.

Chapter 5: Daredevil You

1. Sugar, "DEAR SUGAR, The Rumpus Advice Column
#48: Write Like a Motherfucker," August 19, 2010,
https://therumpus.net/2010/08/dear-sugar-the-rumpus-
advice-column-48-write-like-a-motherfucker

Chapter 6: Women-Only

1. Talking Circle: Fact Sheet, Talking Together, https://
www.learnalberta.ca/content/aswt/talkingtogether/
facilitated_talking_circle_fact_sheet.html

2. Meg Wolitzer, "The Second Shelf: On the Rules of Literary Fiction for Men and Women," *New York Times*,
March 30, 2012, www.nytimes.com/2012/04/01/books/
review/on-the-rules-of-literary-fiction-for-men-and-
women.html.

3. Rebecca Solnit, *Men Explain Things to Me* (Chicago: Haymarket Books, 2014).

4. Dani Shapiro, *Still Writing: The Perils and Pleasures of a Creative Life* (New York: Atlantic Monthly Press, 2013).

5. Olivia Sudjic, *Exposure* (St. Catharines, ON: Peninsula Press, 2018).

6. Kari Paul, "To prevent sexual assault, start with teaching more about sex, educators say," MarketWatch, December 13, 2018, https://www.marketwatch.com/story/want-to-fix-the-metoo-problem-start-with-eliminating-abstinence-only-sex-education-2018-09-19.

Chapter 7: Sisterhoods
1. Mark Nepo, *More Together Than Alone: Discovering the Power and Spirit of Community in Our Lives and in the World* (New York: Atria Books, 2018).

2. The Library of America, "Moved by a Story, Henry James Writes to Edith Wharton for the First Time," *Reader's Almanac*, October 26, 2010, http://blog.loa.org/2010/10/moved-by-story-henry-james-writes-to.html.

Chapter 8: Amplify
1. Kristin Wong, "How to Finally Write Your Nonfiction Book," *New York Times*, December 10, 2018, www.nytimes.com/2018/12/10/smarter-living/how-to-finally-write-your-nonfiction-book.html.

2. Sandra Joseph, *Unmasking What Matters: 10 Life Lessons Learned from 10 Years on Broadway* (Berkeley, CA: She Writes Press, 2018).

About the Author

Brooke Warner is publisher of She Writes Press and SparkPress and president of Warner Coaching Inc. She's an author, coach and memoir teacher, a TEDx speaker, a weekly podcaster, and the former Executive Editor of Seal Press.

Websites:

She Writes Press: www.shewritespress.com
Write-Minded podcast: podcast.shewrites.com
Warner Coaching: www.brookewarner.com
Write Your Memoir in Six Months:
www.writeyourmemoirinsixmonths.com
Magic of Memoir: www.magicofmemoir.com

Find Brooke online:

 warnercoaching   warnercoaching

brooke_warner   warnercoaching

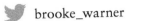 brooke_warner

Author photo © Reenie Raschke

Selected Titles from She Writes Press

She Writes Press is an independent publishing company founded to serve women writers everywhere. Visit us at www.shewrites press.com.

Green-Light Your Book: How Writers Can Succeed in the New Era of Publishing by Brooke Warner. $16.95, 978-1-63152-802-6. A straight-shooting guide to a changing industry that gives indie publishers and authors insight into the current state of publishing, as well as the tools they need to make their books a smashing success.

What's Your Book? A Step-by-Step Guide to Get You from Inspiration to Published Author by Brooke Warner. $12.95, 978-1-938314-00-1. An aspiring author's go-to guide for getting from idea to publication.

The Magic of Memoir: Inspiration for Your Writing Journey by Linda Joy Myers and Brooke Warner. $17.95, 978-1-63152-147-8. Food for the journey and comfort for the soul for memoirists who find themselves in the thick of it, offering interviews with best-selling memoirists and contributions from writers who've gone the distance.

Journey of Memoir: The Three Stages of Memoir Writing by Linda Joy Myers. $22.95, 978-1-938314-26-1. A straightforward, highly effective workbook designed to help memoirists of every level get their story on the page.

Stop Giving it Away: How to Stop Self-Sacrificing and Start Claiming Your Space, Power, and Happiness by Cherilynn Veland. $16.95, 978-1-63152-958-0. An empowering guide designed to help women break free from the trappings of the needs, wants, and whims of other people—and the self-imposed limitations that are keeping them from happiness.

Hedgebrook Cookbook: Celebrating Radical Hospitality by Denise Barr & Julie Rosten. $24.95, 978-1-938314-22-3. Delectable recipes and inspiring writing, straight from Hedgebrook's farmhouse table to yours.

psy. warfare
Shame p106 + Mary Karr
                        p156
outer critics
     p110

CPSIA information can be obtained
at www.ICGtesting.com
Printed in the USA
FSHW021827050319
56118FS

2 370000 663429